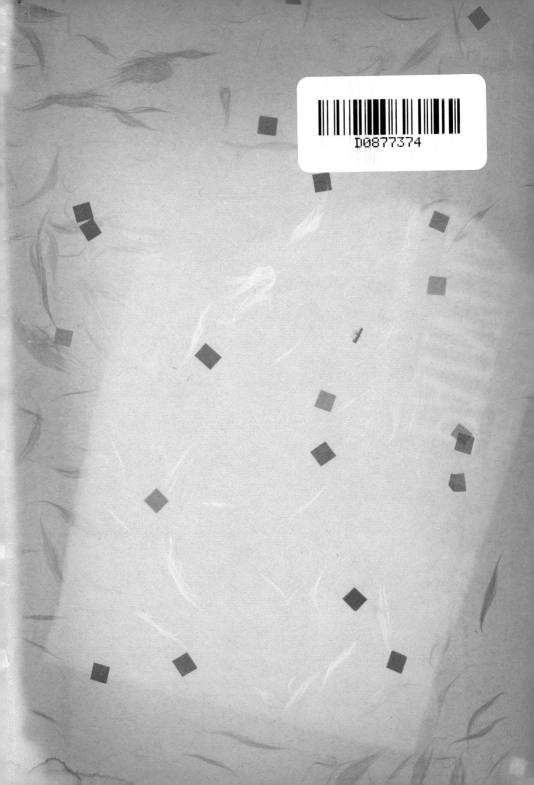

FLOWER ARRANGEMENT ART OF JAPAN

Photograph of the carved and lacquered portrait statue of Sen-no-Rikkiu, 1521–1591, founder of the Enshiu School of Japanese Flower Arrangement.

FLOWER ARRANGEMENT ART OF JAPAN

by

MARY COKELY WOOD

(Popular Reprint Edition)

CHARLES E. TUTTLE COMPANY
RUTLAND VERMONT : TOKYO JAPAN

European Representatives
Continent : BOXERBOOKS, INC., Zurich
British Isles : PRENTICE-HALL INTERNATIONAL INC., London

Published by Charles E. Tuttle Company
Rutland, Vermont & Tokyo, Japan
Editorial offices:
15 Edogawa-cho
Bunkyo-ku, Tokyo

First published, September, 1951
Second edition (revised), December, 1952
Popular edition, eleventh printing, 1961

Printed in Japan

To my husband

Frank Elmer Wood

Preface

The increasing interest in Japanese flower arrangement is the excuse for the appearance of this book. It is meant to be just an introduction to the simplest rules of the line and design arrangement termed Japanese Floral Art as I was taught it in Japan in the late 90's before westernization had touched it.

The purpose of the book is to aid those who would like to learn a floral art built on a few related lines; to be a stimulus to those who like and enjoy a few flowers rather than great masses of them; and above all, to show line drawings of authentic Japanese flower arrangements illustrating all the rules spoken of.

The illustrations are all taken from old floral manuals which have been a constant source of stimulus to myself and my friends. The line drawings are in the traditional black and white "so that the eye is not distracted by color." They are clear, authentic examples of fine arrangements collected by this or that school or individual over a period of many years. Sometimes the best of a collection was published. Because they are line drawings, there is no confusing mass or shadow, and they stand out in sheer stark simplicity and beauty of line, easy to understand.

Three volumes of *rikkwa* (kaleidoscopic view of a landscape) contain outstanding illustrations. These volumes, block printed and hand colored, dated 1684, were compiled by Jiukyushi, who was quite likely a priest; he was a highly gifted floral artist who sought to show by these illustrations the correct principles of *rikkwa*. There is no text but he says in his brief preface that the volumes have "the sole purpose of cultivating the Soul." Undoubtedly they were done as a labor of love.

Added to the study of flower arrangement in Japan have been many years of research in libraries where there were old Japanese floral manuals; there has been much assistance rendered by Japanese friends both in Japan and America to whom I wish to express my sincere thanks. I also wish to thank all those other friends and my husband who have given me much needed advice and encouragement. I also wish to thank Dr. and Mrs. Robert Hall especially for their help and encouragement as well as the many other friends for their advice and friendly interest in compiling this book.

Ann Arbor, Michigan, 1951

Mary Cokely Wood

Contents

List of Illustrations

Introduction

The Study of Japanese Flower Arrangement
and
Its Importance

Every formal, recognized art has its acknowledged form, with rules, regulations, limits, and restrictions within which it moves. All the different phases of these arts which we know best have come from Europe. However, Europe has never had a stylized floral art, with a basis of related lines, such as Japan has.

Flower arrangement, as one of the great arts of Japan, can be traced back to the early fifteenth century, and because of the proficiency which had been achieved at that time, it can be assumed to have been skillfully practiced many years and possibly centuries before that. From the beginning, stylization was inevitable because of the reverence for line and plant habit which is innate in the Japanese race.

The earliest known school of flower arrangement was called Rikkwa. The name comes from two Chinese words, "rik" meaning to build up, and "kwa" meaning flower. A significant explanation of Rikkwa is given by Jiukyushi in the introduction to his exquisitely hand drawn, hand colored, three-volume work, dated 1684, from which the following is taken. "Truly with an inch of water and a foot of tree one produces the effect of a landscape of a thousand leagues of mountains and river. The changes in the life of trees and flowers are mirrored in the space of the *tokonoma*. I have carefully drawn these pictures of the ancient correct flower arrangement for the single purpose of furnishing a means for the cultivation of the soul."

1

Fig. 1

A *rikkwa* which exhibits a beautiful balance of line and contrasting material. The close union of stems at the base gives strength and vitality even to the highly formalized arrangements. The bronze container is simple and adequate; the hint of temple bells is unusual. The material consists of two varieties of pine, *Platycodon,* box, mountain pinks, iris and other handsome leaves, bamboo, and chrysanthemums.

From *Rikkwa Shodo Shu*
by Jiukyushi

2

Fig. 2

An early spring *rikkwa,* quite beautiful in its spreading outlines, in a container of bronze supported by the mythological tiger, often used in stone at the entrance to Buddhist temples. The material consists of pine, box, pussy willows, *Rhodea* and its red berries, large leaves and flowering tree branches.

From *Rikkwa Shodo Shu*
by Jiukyushi

Because of the great amount of material and skill needed to make a Rikkwa arrangement only the nobles could afford them and a more simple art was developed for the average man. This form, called Ikebana, had acquired definite rules by the 12th century. It had been established on the basis of 3–5–7 or more lines with a preference for 3 lines. From this time on until its heyday in the 17th century the rise of the household art of *Ikebana* (which means putting plant life in water) was rapid. It was recognized as an authentic art with its own rules, limitations, and restrictions.

Ikebana was always considered a man's art, so much so that Shunsho, one of the great teachers of the art, wrote: "The study of floral art is a necessity for every man of culture not only to develop the vigor of his mind but to draw out the kindly qualities of his heart."*

From the first, schools have been established to teach the arrangement of flowers. These schools have well trained faculties, extension courses and lectures, books of instruction and there are many thousands of public and private teachers as well as accredited courses in high schools. Japanese Floral Art has an unassailable foundation.

All the different schools and teachers use the same basic fundamentals of line which I shall present in this primer of Japanese flower arrangement. It is the least confusing of methods. After the student has worked out the principles contained in this volume he can easily go on, either to learn how to handle groups of three lines, or to the modern, less restrained styles. In any case he will be enabled to handle any kind of flower material with a better understanding of style.

I have discussed the use of three lines only in order to present the subject as simply as possible. If one can learn to restore "cut" flowers to an appearance of life and growth and project the personality of the flower used, he has learned to do what the painter or sculptor does. The floral artist aims to project a "moment of arrested growth in the life of a living plant." He believes a fine flower arrangement contributes to the cultural atmosphere of the home as much as a fine painting or statue

* M. Revon, De Arte Florali apud Japonenses, 1896, p. 7, note 1.

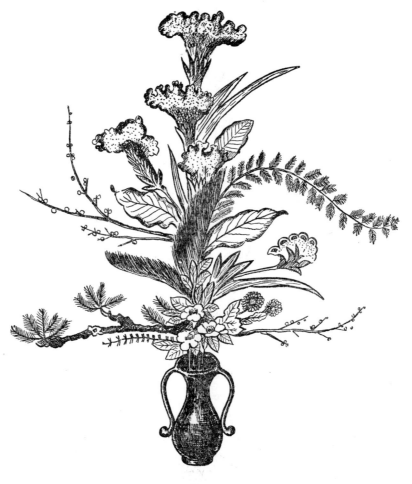

Fig. 3

A *rikkwa*, constructed with *Cryptomeria*, pine, *Celosia*, red plum, camellia, chrysanthemums, iris leaves, fig leaves, and larch in a beautifully proportioned vase with long curved handles. The lower center of the arrangement is well sustained with enough mass for stability, but there is no confusion in the mass and each line flows freely.

From *Rikkwa Shodo Shu*
by Jikyushi

Fig. 4

The floral artist aims to catch a moment of arrested growth in the life
of a living plant. Therefore the arrangement aims to show an idealized
perfection of plant life. This arrangement of chrysathemums in a section
of bamboo shows both of these aims very beautifully.

Fig. 5

Three simple branches of a shrub belonging to the same family as the Michigan holly make a perfect line arrangement, full of life, balance, restraint, and rhythm and yet an easy pattern. Many of America's flowering fruit branches or tree branches can be used in this same style.

can contribute, i.e., it has the momentary beauty that catches the eye but it also has the inner spiritual beauty that holds and also recalls the eye. More than that, it trains the eyes of the family to see new beauties in nature.

Chapter I

Equipment

The equipment for the making of a Japanese flower arrangement is not complicated or expensive except for containers, and does not include much more than one has for the ordinary flower arrangement. In Japan all flower equipment is kept in a suitable closet or store-room. When not holding flowers the containers are not used as objects of decoration. In that country, the actual arrangement is done while the floral artist is seated before the *tokonoma* (alcove) wherein the completed arrangement is to be placed, in order that the flower arrangement may be in perfect harmony with its surroundings.

This idea of complete harmony of surroundings is important in America also. To hold its own any flower arrangement must be made either in the room where it is to be placed, or else with the spot it is to occupy clearly in the mind of the maker of the arrangement. For actual work, a dining table spread with a sheet of oilcloth for the protection of the table and for tidiness has no equal.

There should be pails to hold flower material overnight in deep water. In the winter when evergreens need thorough cleansing in soapy water in complete immersion, the laundry tubs can be used.

A large pitcher of water to fill the container when the arrangement has been completed is convenient, though the handy tap is sometimes easier. A roll of paper toweling is more useful to us than the 40 inch square of cloth the Japanese use.

To protect the fine finish of tables, pieces of felt should be cut and glued to the bottom of heavy bronzes and heavy pottery containers.

As for tools, a good pair of pruning shears, heavy enough to cut through a good sized branch, and made of steel that will take and keep a good edge, is a necessity; so is a sharp jackknife, and a hammer to

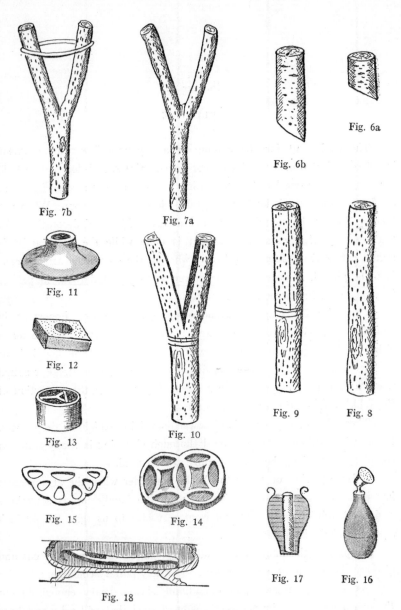

Fig. 7b

Fig. 7a

Fig. 6b

Fig. 6a

Fig. 11

Fig. 12

Fig. 13

Fig. 10

Fig. 9

Fig. 8

Fig. 15

Fig. 14

Fig. 17

Fig. 16

Fig. 18

Figs. 6–18

Necessary equipment for *Ikebana*. [Sketches by Mina Winslow]

bruise the ends of branches and drive in wedges. A small pair of scissors to snip off leaves is a comfort. Added to these, many fine containers of all sorts of shapes and sizes give freedom to one who arranges flowers. I'd like to emphasize the fact that one never regrets the money put into a Japanese bronze flower container because it is practically unbreakable, constantly usable and always an inspiration.

It is well to keep on hand a number of short lengths of branches of various diameters, from 1/4 to 3/4 inches. These branches can be cut into any needed length to serve as wedges. Sometimes discarded stems of whatever flower material is being used can be utilized for wedges, but often flower stems are too soft and slender for this purpose. Firm, stout stems are best. Wedges should be cut straight across one end and slantingly across the other. (Figs. 6a-6b) Smooth off every little bit of roughness on a wedge before trying to insert it, otherwise it will not hold firmly.

Whenever it is possible a *komi* alone should be used to hold the stems because it makes such a neat strong stay. A *komi* (Figs. 8 and 13) is a slender but firm length of branch cut the diameter of the container and laid across at right angles to the *kubari*.

The *kubari* is the simple means by which the stems in a Japanese flower arrangement are held firmly erect at the angle desired. The most common and effectual *kubari* (Fig. 7a) is a forked twig just such as Johnny used to use for a sling shot. The forks should be as even as possible, not too far apart, with the stem straight and smooth about 1/4 to 3/8 inch in diameter. The *kubari* is fitted into the top of an erect container about an inch below the rim, or into heavy iron rings (Fig. 13) for a basin container, or into a tin tube (Fig. 17) which can be inserted into a breakable container. Many containers are too smooth inside to readily be fitted with a *kubari*. These can be smeared for the depth of an inch with a pottery cement or heavy glue that when dried will make a rough surface so that the *kubari* will not slip about. This coating of cement should be put in about an inch below the rim.

The stems of the flower arrangement are to be inserted in the fork and held there firmly by means of the *komi* or by wedges. A well fitted, medium-sized *kubari* will last a long time. The best material to make them of is of apple, willow or peach. A too-wide fork may be made smaller by wiring the fork to make a smaller aperture. The wiring must be done before fitting the *kubari*. (Fig. 7b)

If forked twigs are out of the question, take a length of a branch about 3/8 of an inch in diameter, split it about half the length of the diameter of the container to be used and wrap several strands of fine wire around the branch so that the split will not extend farther (Fig. 9). One can also buy a yard of round rattan from a chair caning shop and use in this same way. A yard of rattan will furnish all the *kubari* needed for a long time.

The purpose of the *kubari* is to get the close union of stems at the water's edge and for some inches above, and to hold these stems at whatever angle is desired. The *komi* or wedges hold the stems firmly in the fork of the *kubari* (without any visible support since the *kubari* will be below the surface of the water) in the center of the container. The stems of the flower arrangement firmly and invisibly held in the center of the mouth of the container give a strong sense of vitality and animation so that the arrangement seems alive, and appears to spring from the container of its own volition.

In the early summer time when baskets are often used, or in the case of easily breakable containers, a cylindrical tube of tin or bronze (bamboo in Japan) is made and inserted in the container. (Fig. 17) The tube should be made about an inch less in diameter and an inch less in height than the container. The *kubari* is fitted in this tube and the arrangement made in it before it is slipped into the container. The water should cover a *kubari*.

For flower holders in basins there are a number of useful and effectual ways to hold stems erect and closely united at the base. The Japanese were not so limited in flower holders for basins as they were for erect containers, where the method of holding the stems firmly was not exposed. The more odd or quaint the form of the fastener seen, the more charm was added to the arrangement as a whole. In cases where real service was

12

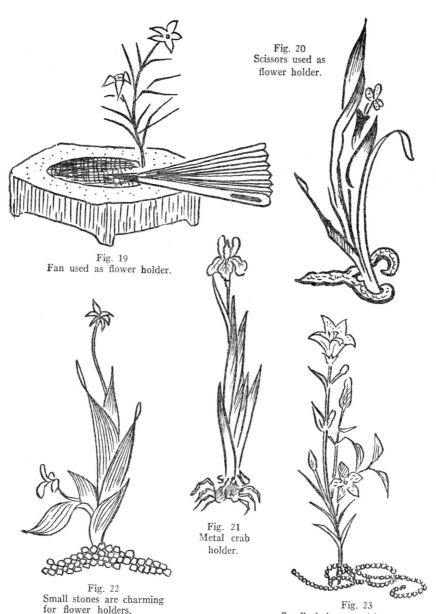

Fig. 20
Scissors used as
flower holder.

Fig. 19
Fan used as flower holder.

Fig. 21
Metal crab
holder.

Fig. 22
Small stones are charming
for flower holders.

Fig. 23
Small chain may either cover up
an ugly holder or be used
as a holder.

Figs. 19–23
Examples of Flower Holders for Basins.

13

demanded for heavy branches in large bronze basins, the useful heavy iron ring was most efficient. In a large basin three stones interestingly weathered and waterworn were often added to make a *keikwa* or landscape scene. Unless the flower basin is sufficiently large, such an arrangement is apt to look cramped and trivial.

I have found that heavy iron nuts (Fig. 12) painted black are very convenient because they can be found in all sizes and shapes. Some have a flange or collar such as Figure 11 shows. The collar adds weight. The small square nuts may, if desired, be hidden by small stones, though usually the water, especially over a dark bottom, is enough disguise. Heavy lead pin blocks can also be easily purchased, but I find it very difficult to get that close, tight union of stems above the water line with pin blocks. Lightweight holders may be securely attached to the bottom of a basin by dipping the pin block into hot melted parafin and placing it wherever desired. The parafin when cold holds the pin block very securely in place and lasts a long time. The right flower fastener which has weight and is inconspicuous is quite often the product of some one's ingenuity. The advantage of the iron nuts is that the stems can be kept more tightly together because wedges can be inserted to keep them from spreading apart, an advantage when building a good design. The wedges should never protrude above the nut or any holder used. Small stones can be used to conceal the nut or other holder, but in classic design nothing else should ever be used to conceal a flower fastener. Needless to say, the very small stones seen in pictures of Japanese arrangements cannot, alone, hold stems firmly enough. They are merely accessory to the fact.

The Japanese used many odd lead or bronze crabs, also fish and turtle shapes for flower holders in basins and occasionally one can pick these up. They delighted also in collecting stones from well known spots of beauty in their islands. They used red stones in the autumn, black in the winter, green in the spring and white in the summer to lend a charming air of credibility and suggestion to arrangements in sand basins or pottery bowls. These shallow basins are used much more in the spring and summer than at other seasons because at these times the sight of an open expanse of water is refreshing and suggestive.

A small spray to sprinkle the completed arrangement and give it dewy freshness should be among the equipment. The spray may be a rubber one from the dime store (Fig. 16) or a fine brass syringe.

Chapter II
Before Plant Material is Selected

Every Japanese flower arrangement presents a new problem to an American, a problem which only thought and time and practice will routinize. For instance, "Where shall we put our flower arrangement?" is a common question *after* the arrangement has been completed. That question in Japan has never been brought up for in that country from very primitive times a place of honor has been built into the best room or rooms of every home. This place is a small recess called a *tokonoma*, a space three feet by six feet raised about four inches above the floor. In the *tokonoma*, which is the focus of the room, are placed all the movable, decorative objects of the room, the flower arrangement, a hanging picture and occasionally a small carving.

The *tokonoma*, like the rest of the room, has plain, neutral-colored walls. Its size gives plenty of space for the freely flowing-upward-and-outward rhythms of the *ikebana*. The soft coloring of Japanese rooms makes an ideal background for any art object, and the height of the rooms varies so little that the outer limits of the *tokonoma* are ideal for those *objets d'art* to form in themselves a beautiful ensemble in their traditional grouping.

In America, if we are to get the most value from a flower arrangement considered as a work of art, we must consider these same things; a plain, neutral-colored background; space for perspective; and an absence of trivial, unrelated objects. Given these conditions, a tall arrangement in a high-ceilinged room becomes a part of the room; a short, bunchy, bouquet, a matter of color only, in the same room is often so overwhelmed as to be lost, or becomes just a patch of color in the midst of a crowded table.

The modern room, with its sense of spaciousness and soft coloring, is ideal for a Japanese flower arrangement, but even its distinction of

16

Fig. 24

A tall, sweeping arrangement of plum and camellia in a large bronze. The rounded base scallop and scallop border pick up the petal scallop while the flare of the container harmonizes with the curve of the main stem. The shape and quaintness of the handles also fit in well. The arrangement is tall enough to dominate an entire wall space. The camellia is probably a deep pink or red, the plum red or white. A very distinguished *ikebana* with its sharp angles, long *nemoto* and flowing beauty of line. It is the pattern shown in Figure 92.

17

suavely flowing lines can be lost in a crowded room filled with brilliant coloring and many distracting lines and forms. On the other hand no other kind of a flower arrangement can give the distinctive charm to a beautiful drawing room that a classic Japanese flower arrangement can because its height and style enables it to mingle its lines with the lines of the room and to return elegance for elegance.

For instance, there was an unforgettable loveliness in an arrangement of the brown branches and yellow flowers of witch hazel, placed against a background of delicate green. The branches lacked leaves, but they still had the nutlike fruits of the preceding year as well as the elfin flowers. It assumed significance because of its height, three feet six inches, and because it was the focus of two rooms seen through an archway. It seemed to fill all the space between the two doorways with its vibrant rhythms flowing off into space.

A Japanese flower arrangement should never be put casually on a piano or table but should be silhouetted on a table or chest against a wall at a good eye-height. Thus it can have background. There should never be anything near it to call the eye away from its lovely flowing lines. Displayed thus, it has no difficulty in maintaining its own dynamic beauty.

Much of the distinction of such an arrangement comes from the careful selection of the container. The harmony between flower material and flower container must be such that while one does not forget that there is a flower container he is lost in admiration of the arrangement as a whole and its value to the room.

The container, therefore must be dark and solid looking enough for a substantial base, but not so heavy as to destroy the balance of the harmony of the design as a whole.

To sum it all up, we must plan to place a Japanese flower arrangement with as much care as we hang a fine painting, in regard to background, lighting and eye height, in a place where it assumes significance. We heighten its significance by planning beforehand to make its relationship to the room in regard to color, style, height, and line as perfect and harmonious as possible. Its vibrant vitality will then fill the room.

Chapter III

Plant Material

In Japan, it was necessary to use the seasonal and regional tree and plant material for the altar arrangements which so long antedated the flower arrangements in the home. During the years between 552 and 1000 A. D. while the altar style was being crystallized, and probably for many years succeeding, there were no nurseries, no greenhouses, and perhaps even no flower gardens in our sense of the word. The votive offerings had to be seasonal and regional. Therefore the floral artists had no traditions of standardized lengths when they came to make *Ikebana* in the 10th or 11th century.

There is no doubt that from very early times people in those islands stuck flowers into some vessel or other as all peoples do now. That style, if it may be called a style, was called *Nage-ire,* "flowers thrown into a vase." But that feeling for form and style and ceremony which has always characterized the Japanese, beside their real love for flowers, demanded that flowers too should be treated with dignity and reverence.

The altar arrangements had always been tall. They were from four feet upward in the 10th century. Today one may find an altar arrangement fifteen feet high if the occasion demands it. It was natural then that the *ikebana* should follow the tradition of height. Height gave freedom to make lovely lines, to show plant identity, and even to exaggerate many natural effects, as in music we accent certain notes to make a rhythm more pronounced. (Fig. 28)

For example, it was deemed important to show the drooping characteristic of the forsythia (Fig. 29), or the very pronounced erectness of a species of iris (Fig. 27). In other words, each species as well as each genus had personal identity which we call plant habit. This identity became most emphatic in the peak of the plant's season. The natural result was that in

19

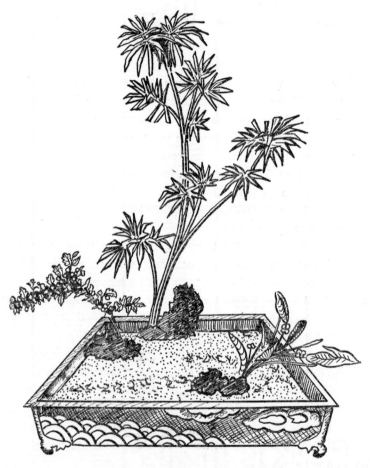

Fig. 25

Keikwa or flower landscape of bamboo, chrysanthemum and *Nuphar* with weatherworn stones in a large bronze basin engraved with waves and clouds. Each group has a trilinear, triangular form and the three groups as a whole also present a tridimensional form. There is a thin layer of sand over about half the basin; this is also triangular.

Fig. 26

A very chastely formal arrangement of iris in a tall, straight bamboo container. Its tall leaves and two blossoms with one bud show the austerity of habit of this species. The arrangement has style, elegance and height. The cut-in base of the container takes away from the appearance of weight and mass, adds to the height and duplicates, in a way, the effect of the two flowers at the top.

Fig. 29

This arrangement, with
erect stem and droop-
ing branch. Shows the
common habit of the
forsythia. Its height is
four times the height
of the container from
the water line. It has
a very satisfying pro-
jection of personality.
Whenever possible,, tree
or shrub branches were
cut to extend to the
bottom of the contain-
er.

Fig. 27

This formal iris is
three times the height
of the container. The
whole arrangement has
an elegant simplicity.

Fig. 28

An arrangement of *Evonymus*
where the main stem is three
and one-half times the height
of the attractive bamboo root
container.

classic *Ikebana* seasonal and regional material has always been considered the best material to use, because it keeps the mind "in tune with nature."

The flora of Japan is one of the richest in the world, not only in genera and species, but in luxuriance. The floral artists could, and did, try out for century after century flower material that stood the test for style, character, personality, individuality, and for lasting a long time after arrangement. More than that, the material had to be a common part of the landscape. It was never exotic or foreign.

The word *hana* which we loosely translate "flower" includes all kinds of plant material from grasses to trees; the widely varying materials may be seen from the following incomplete list—incomplete because unnecessary in this book to list more than we may be more or less familiar with: Evergreens, including pines, cedars, *Cryptomeria,* cypress, yew, junipers, larch, and the wide-leaved evergreens such as rhododendrons, azaleas, Andromeda, camellias, *Evonymus,* gardenias, *Podocarpus,* box holly, are most used of this group. The flowering fruit trees, the Wisteria, loquat, tree and herbaceous peonies, witch hazel, *Sambucus, Deutsia,* clematis, roses, willows, *Nandina,* forsythia, and bush clover are common trees and shrubs frequently used. Among the flowers are chrysanthemums, iris, *Rhodea,* morning glories, asters, *Lobelia, Polygonum, Aconite, Celosia* (a common plant in temple gardens), *Dianthus,* narcissus, *Nuphar,* cannas, *Lysimachia,* lotus, *Hypericum, Funkia,* poppies, *patrinia* (Ladies' flower), *Begonia Evansiana, Cypripedium,* dandelion, *Astilbe, Primula, Hemoracallis,* calendulas, *Platycodon,* lilies of many varieties, and the popular and common *Aspidistra.* To this list are added many grasses, reeds, rushes and *Equisetum.* Each of these plant materials has been proved adequate by the "cut and try" methods of centuries.

Chrysanthemums, willows, *Nandina, Rhodea,* iris, roses, *Eupatorium,* and *Hibiscus* were most common among what were ranked as "flowers of the four seasons." The changing seasons and the great abundance of material prevented any monotony in flower arrangements, and also developed skill in the use of materials which could be used again and again in different patterns during the season when each was most itself, just as a

Fig. 32
These branches of peach
are three and one-half
times the height of the
container.

Fig. 31

Fig. 30
The *Cypripedium* is three
and one half times the
height of the container.

Fig. 34
The Oriental poppy
is two and three-
fourths times the
the height of the
container.

Fig. 33
A formal arrange-
ment of chrys-
anthemums twice
the height of the
container.

painter can make drawing after drawing of some object until he "gets the feeling" of the object. (Figs. 50, 76, 85, 86, 95, 136)

We get this seasonal and regional feeling from a familiar landscape, but not necessarily (especially now when great greenhouses and nurseries are so common) from flowers alone. We should however emphasize seasonal material as much as possible, especially that from our gardens.

In Japan the idea of a garden is still a landscape without flowers, except for seasonal tree and shrub flowering, which is a by-product of landscape design. A shrub or tree flowering in a Japanese garden is there because the particular shape of that tree or shrub-growth is the one fitted to carry out the landscape design, not primarily because of its flowers.

The Japanese flower arrangement therefore contains many ideas that we do not embody or even think of embodying in a bouquet. The Japanese artist takes from nature as a whole such plants for arrangement as he conceives to have values, or relationships suggestive of human experience in connection with time, season, place, emotion, and symbolism, as well as the physical characteristics demanded. The scope of material used has made tradition play a great part in the arrangement of flowers in Japan, in addition to the background of the religious floral art.

The symbolism expressed by the flowers on the altar had its effect on *Ikebana*, because the trees and flowers retained this symbolism of whatever mystic virtue they were imbued with. Lotus in all lands has been symbolical of purity. In Japan evergreens, especially pines, have been symbolical of long life because they so successfully withstand all the vicissitudes of life. The chrysanthemum in both China and Japan is symbolical of immortality; the bamboo of endurance and devotion to duty, because it will bend but not break, and will stand defiantly in a place it likes; the plum of courage, because it blossoms in the snow; the iris blade of patriotism, because of its likeness to a sword blade.

Juniper or pine, symbolical of long life, in a bronze engraved with storks, also symbolical of long life, conveys to the birthday child the wish that he may live a thousand happy years. This *ikebana* very happily illustrates the idea of human relationship, emotion, symbolism, and a flower

Fig. 36

Though this arrangement looks very tall, it is only one and a half times the length of the boat-shaped container. It is a charming arrangement of spring iris.

Fig. 35

An arrangement of fall iris indicated by the drooping irregularity of the leaves. It is more than three times the height of the bamboo container, which has been cut into an eared and legged shape making evident the long and short lines of container and material.

Fig. 38

An arrangement of *Funkia* flowers and leaves which is three and one half times the height of the root bamboo container. The buds and flowers and root scars all tie together, while the squatty shape responds to the rounded leaf shapes, the tall flower stems to the straight sides.

Fig. 37

"The Three Friends of Winter" —the bamboo, symbolical of devotion, the plum of courage, and the pine of long life. This is the traditional New Year's flower arrangement in Japan. It is five times the height of the simple, dignified bronze container.

27

material that has no real season or region, brought together in a traditional design that has no limit as to season, time, or place. This is an example of how all such ideas may be crystallized in a perenially beautiful tradition.

Again, a branch of cherry (Fig. 39) displayed in the *tokonoma* may recall to the family not only the lovely vision of the tree from which it was taken but also many annual "flower excursions." These are not picnics but seasonal visits to local or distant places for the sole purpose of "viewing the flowers" (*hana-mi-yuku*). Families may spend an entire day, monthly, just to "get their fill of the flowers," as an old proverb has it. I can never forget a certain huge old cherry tree in Kyoto and my astonishment in seeing about 5,000 people enjoying its mystic beauty one moonlit night.

The triangular and tridimensional form of a cherry blossom arrangement, its height, and its careful detail in regard to each leaf and flower, presented a radiant beauty. It also recalled to everyone who saw it many charming occasions and experiences as well as the very tree from which this branch had been cut.

A short-stemmed bunch of cherry blossoms alone could not recall or suggest so many vivid human emotions or experiences; nor can any dozen roses, no matter how costly or how triumphantly perfect, present to the eye or to the mind the swift succession of thought, mental picture and human association that this tall arrangement of cherry branches suggested. The beauty of any Japanese flower arrangement is taken for granted, but each arrangement must have, besides the beauty, a spiritual element sufficiently suggestive to evoke a response from the observer. It is obvious therefore that the flower material must be from a tree or plant that is common and well known, or at least similar to one we know, to get this spiritual effect.

There were various ways by which the spiritual element was made more apparent. Besides the flower arrangement, a *kakemono* (hanging scroll) was often placed in the *tokonoma* and perhaps a piece of fine carving, showing how the three fine arts have been, and are today, associated, as they were associated on the altars at the beginning of the floral art.

These three objects had to suggest a subtle harmony flowing from one to another. Many of these harmonies became traditional. For in-

Fig. 39

A beautiful *keikwa* arrangement of branches of an old cherry tree. Cherry blossoms are rarely arranged with other material. The height of this arrangement is only about one and a third times the length of the basin. The effect is that of a very beautiful landscape.

Fig. 40

An arrangement of willow and camellia is popular for a felicitous occasion. The arrangement, four times the height of the bronze container, is very stately and graceful. Its curves over and over again respond to the curves of the container.

stance, in one *tokonoma* was hung a long narrow picture depicting a mountain stream rushing down a ravine to a pool at the bottom. Near the bottom of the picture, which reached almost to the floor, was an arrangement of iris in a bronze container on a small stand. The arrangement was set a little to the right of the *kakemono* so that the artist's signature was not hidden. The container was a flat cone resting on the crest of a wave and the flowers seemed to rise out of the water itself. This whole grouping was very suggestive of a clump of iris that might naturally grow on the edge of a small pool. The carving was a black wooden one of "the smiling Buddha." The *tokonoma* as a whole presented a richly harmonious ensemble full of suggestion and association.

To a race "in tune with nature" every landscape had its associations. To the Japanese, inured to hardship, the sight of pines, twisted, distorted, dwarfed by the elements, clinging with all their might to the rocky face of a cliff, or standing on a windswept ridge silhouetted against the sky, fairly shouted, "Never mind the going, just keep on." Standing thus, century after century, evergreens were associated with courage as well as long life. They lived on in spite of elemental rages. They did not merely decorate the landscape. The old floral masters, many of whom in their early life had been soldiers, loved evergreens and used them in flower arrangements as well as in their gardens. Evergreens, especially pines, are the great background in Japan, of the scenery, the garden, and the floral art.

If we desire to develop a real floral art in America, the material that we use for flower arrangement should have the same qualities demanded in Japan, that is, it must be common, easy to get, simple, expressive, and with the ability to stand up well after an arrangement has been made. One has only to look through old Japanese floral manuals to see how much variation, grace, and simplicity without monotony (Fig. 42) is shown by the use of what we consider extremely ordinary material, e.g. elderberry and dandelion in an arrangement projecting the plant personalities expressively and charmingly, as well as apparently unrestrainedly.

In Japan, the use of seasonal and regional material made flower arrangements a part of the family routine, an integral part of family life.

Fig. 41

The pine is the great background of the scenery, the garden, and the floral art in Japan. This is a magnificient arrangement and use of one branch, an unusual one with a large fungus. The artist did not attempt to cut the branch but shows the full value, so suggestive of many loved spots.

Fig. 43
Pussy willow
from a nearby
lake.

Fig. 42
Sambucus and dandelion from the open woods.

Fig. 44
Funkia from the cutting garden of the home.

33

They became bulletins, as it were. They told whether the family was poor or prosperous; they acted as a calendar, telling the season of the year, the month, often the day of the month· they told the region, mountain or plain, the lake or the little flower shop, or the cutting garden about the home; they told the special news, a birthday, a wedding, a coming of age, a death or an occasion for congratulation, a journey or the arrival of guests; every event in the home was heralded by a flower arrangement. Flowers that were given by friends were distinguished by being put into hanging receptacles so that they might be looked up to.

One of the most common and traditional of the year's calendar arrangements is that of the New Year's festival which uses the "three friends of winter," the pine for longevity, the plum for courage, the bamboo for endurance, all three seasonal and regional almost everywhere in Japan; congratulatory and linked with many associations, all stand up well and make a beautiful arrangement in any of many possible combinations (Fig. 141).

An illustration taken from one of the old floral manuals shows how the last bit of value could be extracted from the most simple of flower material, two small shrubby twig-like branches, the least capable (since they had no leaves or blossoms) of any material—from an American point of view—of expressing any great interest or emotion; but see what these little branches tell to the knowing observer.

The two little branches were hung in a small basket on the post of the *tokonoma*. A long narrow tablet was hung on the post behind the basket to prevent it from marring the finish of the post. On this tablet is a flowing-line-pattern suggestive of water. The branches have been put into a suspended container, a fish basket, again suggestive of water. The branches therefore undoubtedly were from some shrubs, perhaps beach plums, growing on a bank above the water, and because they have no leaves, it is early spring.

It is plainly evident that the family was not rich, but this simple little flower arrangement speaks of the coming of spring as its leaf buds slowly open as if it were a branch of a great tree speaking to the *daimyo* himself.

34

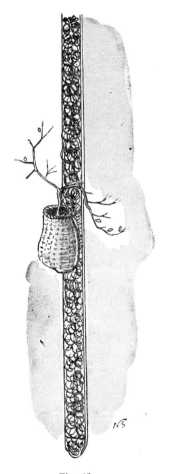

Fig. 45

The most simple flower arrangement, from an American point of view, that could be; and yet as its leaf buds slowly open, it speaks of the coming of spring as plainly as if it were a branch of a great tree speaking to the *daimyo* himself.

The subtle harmony of tablet, container, branch, and suspended position which allowed the beauty of the sweeping character of the beach plum to show, are all filled with suggestion, animation, rhythm and vitality. The arrangement as a whole is dynamic and alive, yet no flower arrangement could be more simple and appealingly suggestive as day by day its leaf buds open.

Such suggested spiritual values and actual beauty were the aim of all floral artists whether the material had the angularity of the pine or the austerity of the iris; the glowing splendor of maple trees in autumn, or the wide, glossy, green leaves of the *Aspidistra;* the radiant colors of the chrysanthemum flowers and the cool beauty of their leaves, or the length and movement of the jointed grass (*Miscanthus,* Fig. 140). Each plant or tree has some dominating spiritual and physical element which is important and pleasant to emphasize, something that is not to be taken into consideration in standardized, unnatural perfection of masses of horti-cultural material.

The floral artist could, and did, take advantage of the incidental or the natural ugliness or beauty of a plant, or any fantastic quirk of nature, and make it say something interesting. (Fig. 136) He knew that nature, left to herself, is intent on perpetuation of species rather than perfection, but nature in herself has beauty in every stem and does not need a mass of material and color to prove it.

Therefore the artist aimed to project the personality, spiritual and physical, of whatever material he was dealing with, in as charming a way as possible, in the season of the year when it was at its best.

From all points of view the Japanese floral artist's idea as regards material and its arrangement is based on common sense and beauty, derived from a close observance of nature. One of the most important of his ideas is the matter of height in an arrangement. As any fashion magazine demonstrates, style, and elegance, and flowing beauty of design depend considerably on height. An *ikebana* in Japan is never thought of as consisting of plant material *and* container, but as a single unit of design, with the result that height assumes value, or, in other words,

36

Fig. 46

Aspidistra leaves are extremely popular for flower arrangement in Japan because they are common and easy to work into all sorts of interesting, even fantastic shapes. They are long lasting because evergreen. Here the curl of the leaf features the curl of the handles and cloud motif of the container.

Fig. 47

In the spring maple branches are full of life. The cut-in base of the container corresponds to the cut-in of the leaves.

Fig. 48

It was startling to see our familiar cabbage allowed to grow loosely and viewed as an exotic plant. The tiny button chrysanthemums are a strong contrast to the big leaves.

the stems have to be cut long in order to make an effective arrangement.

Height, which means the cutting of long stems or branches, lessens the scope of flower material by excluding much that is short or insignificant; it also excludes soft-stemmed plants which are of much more value as charming spots of color in a garden. But while it excludes material of this kind it includes much other material, such as tree branches of many kinds as mentioned in the incomplete list given earlier in this chapter. These tree branches make sweeping arrangements in the classic art forms and express and suggest a great richness in nature. They can bring tranquillity into a room and fairly sing of the beauty of forest and plain, the teeming summer, the abundant fruit harvests, the swamp and the pine woods. They can remove the cramping feeling of walls much more effectively than a short bunch of flowers in a low dish.

In the early spring a most lovely *ikebana* can be made of the brilliant red osier stems which are so good to use for practice in line designs. Besides that, in a warm room it is not long before little shoots of green leaves pop out from each joint to envelop the whole arrangement in a veil of tender green. While the Japanese disapproved of forcing flower material (they had no need to force material), we, in a different climate and under different conditions and in many places with less opportunity to secure seasonal and regional material, may be pardoned if we force tree and shrub branches. Indeed it is almost necessary to do this if we wish to keep constantly at work on stems for practice in line arrangements.

After we have made a fairly satisfying line arrangement of forsythia, pussy willow, or red osier, it should be left for a week or two to leaf out, or come into bloom; or just to be enjoyed, or to be studied and corrected. The comments and criticism of family and friends are often interesting and helpful. There is a great difference in practice in arranging stems without leaves, stems with leaves, stems with flowers only, and stems with both leaves and flowers. It takes all kinds of stems for practice if we are really to learn how to draw designs with stems.

During the early spring there is a wealth of opening tree and blossom buds which give a thrill to the arranger of stems. The silver leaf poplar

Fig. 49

The height of this perfect lotus arrangement is not quite twice the
length of the basin, which, in spite of its rectangular shape, throws
back a feeling akin to the large wide-open leaves. The arrangement has a fine balance, spacing, strength, and beauty.

is most delicately beautiful when its leaf buds are just beginning to open; the early flowering wild plum is lovely when arranged either by itself or with pine; there are the red leaves of the low growing *Viburnum*, the small red-velvet leaves of the white oak, and the lovely yellow leaves and tassels of the black oak, and the dramatic and brilliant young hickory stems.

Young maple branches with their small red leaves on perky upturned tips will energize any room quite as much as if they were blossoms. Branches of the flowering currant are charming and sweet smelling. Burr oak is a most sharply dramatic material with its angular, ridged branches, on which after a week or so in the house, come little tufts of green velvet leaves, a great contrast to the stiff hard stems. The *Evonymus alata*, its feminine counterpart, is almost as interesting (Fig. 29). Late in the fall the witch hazel, with its nubby little nutlets of the preceding year and delicate starlike yellow blossoms, even though it lacks leaves is a striking addition to a room. The alders and birches are charmingly usable two seasons of the year, spring and fall, and there is the really stunning sumac.

To add variety or interest to flowerless or leafless branches, it is always permissible to use a little bunch of small flowers in place of the shortest stems. This bunch of flowers is called a *nejime,* or sometimes an *ashirai.* (Fig. 97)

In the classic *ikebana,* the Japanese prefer to use only one kind of flower material; if one does not have enough long material of one kind a *nejime* may be very useful. Two branches of pine or juniper (either of which will last several weeks) may have a succession of *nejime,* each containing a different variety of flowers. One may use in this way tall stems of privet with red zinnias, or dahlias. Dahlias too, if not too large, are one of the most lovely materials to use in many different designs. Michigan holly may be used with evergreens or the holly may be used alone if the stems are long and well berried. (Fig. 5)

There are many lovely roadside plants—milkweeds, Queen Anne's lace, *Eupatorium,* Joe Pye weed, *Liatris'* purple stalks, cardinal flowers, *Scutellaria, Pentstemon, Lysimachia* (swamp candles), tules, reeds, bul-

40

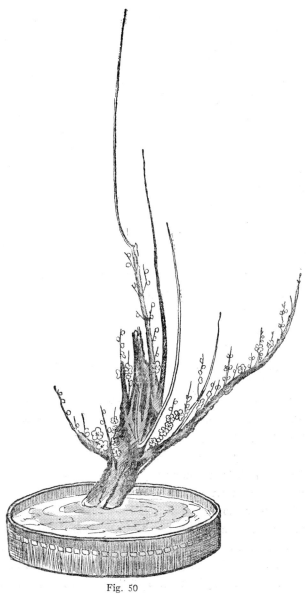

Fig. 50

Once in **a** lifetime perhaps, such a branch as **this might**
come into one's possession. Its simplicity is striking.

rushes, pickerel weed, *Equisetum,* large thistles, and young pale green-and-orchid teasels. In all cases, when selecting material see that the leaves are all as perfect as possible.

Large double flowers are not a good choice for Japanese flower arrangements. They are too heavy for line arrangements. As the illustrations show, in the case of peonies a single one may be used, but not one of the largest size; the arrangement then has to be made large enough to take such a flower, and its place in the design is carefully selected. If a plant is thickly leaved, the leaves are most carefully thinned out after the arrangement has been made so that each leaf has its definite place in the design. (Fig. 69)

On hot days in summer, an arrangement of snow-on-the-mountain or an arrangement of water plants in a basin that can show a large expanse of water is pleasantly cooling and becomes part of the cultured, ordered atmosphere of the room. (Fig. 140) In late summer, fall and winter gladiolas may be arranged in a great many interesting designs in both erect and basin containers.

In winter, when one needs color and cheer, an arrangement of ever-green and holly fits in with American custom; or in early fall, in place of the popular bunch of bittersweet, use one beautifully grown, fully berried spray with one or two of English ivy or *Philodendron* in a hanging container or wall pocket. The ivy will grow and the bittersweet retain its sharply contrasting effect all winter, while the line arrangement will satisfy the aesthetic sense.

To sum up the discussion of material, though one *can* use in an *ikebana* the choicest flowers money can buy, they do not in themselves assure one that an arrangement made from them will give as much satisfaction as can be gained from more simple and common material. It is not horticultural perfection or exotic blooms that insure the exquisite beauty of an arrangement that will linger longest in the mind, but it is the ability to project in an apparently natural, artless unrestrained style a material that may not seem distinctive yet can stir a thrill in the spectator.

Such an arrangement, no matter what the material, is a dynamic, vital, and spiritual force in a room.

Chapter IV

Containers

One of the great beauties of an authentic art is its simplicity, which in Japanese floral art involves common sense, balance, proportion, and uncrowded effects as well as a beauty that is obviously appealing. Nowhere is this better shown than in the aesthetic feeling that makes a unit of flower material and container, an important part of which is the rightness of the container as well as its intrinsic charm.

There is no nation that has produced flower vases so outstanding in beauty of design as has Japan, though the museums and stores are full of ancient and modern vase forms of all nations, vases of size, dignity, color and smoothly flowing lines. The Japanese love of floral art has been a constant stimulus to their craftsmen, whose fertile imaginations have kept pace with their facile fingers. Every ornament and design in a Japanese flower container (Fig. 49) has been exactly right for the shape and form to which it was applied. Whenever handles have been put on a vase, those handles (Fig. 2) have been designed as a part of the pattern. As a result, Japanese flower containers are utterly satisfying, not only as beautiful forms but as vases whose primary use is to hold flowers. The rim line is clear and simple; the color is rich, but subdued and varied, and adapted to the probable future use of the piece.

It has been a tradition in Japan that flowers should be inserted only in a container designed for flowers; this is in accordance with the dignity of the art. Flowers have not been put into a household utensil even if more than a hundred years have passed since it has been used as a utensil, by any devotee of the art.

Until modern flower arrangement and Western influence came, the makers of flower vases ordinary kept to the dark, rich colors of bronze, or they used dark pottery colored like the earth. The precedent was the

Fig. 51

This beautiful arrangement of *nanten* berry branches and *nejime* of *Aspidistra* and narcissus in a calthrop-shaped basin illustrates many of the rules of a fine arrangement. The sharp corners of the basin respond to the sharply pointed tips of the leaves, while the rounded corners of the stand beneath respond to the curve of the heaven line and the curves of the leaves. The berries are emphasized by the pattern on the sides of the container. The flare of the heaven line in both groups is the same. The larger group is *Yang*, the smaller *Ying*. The space between the groups is called the "fishes' way."

T'ang bronze of the first altar vase. Bronze and pottery containers were solid, earthy-looking, unbreakable, or nearly so, easily lasting several hundred years because a fine container was a household treasure destined to become an heirloom. (Fig. 24) In spite of their substantial nature they were not over-heavy and the materials made a very attractive contrast to the delicate blossoms of the plant material. (Fig. 70)

The lines of the plant material flowed out from the containers as naturally and beautifully as plant or tree life rises from its natural locality, the rich dark earth. (Fig. 44) All plant material, whether flowers or tree branches, grasses or water plants, looks settled and at home in the dark bronze or pottery containers, just as a richly colored painting looks best and at home in a frame of subdued tone. No painting looks happy in a big white or orchid colored frame. Such colors kill the painting. It cannot hold its own. Nor can a flower material stand out in dignity and maintain itself in a container that is an eye catcher.

The purpose of both frame and container is to hold the picture or flower material as harmoniously and unobtrusively as possible so that, though one is conscious of a frame or container, the eye is conscious only of a single unit of design. The container sinks into the background. On the critical choice of the right container hangs the success or failure of the Japanese flower arrangement. The use of fine containers emphasizes the exquisite simplicity of the Japanese floral art. (Fig. 68)

In looking through old Japanese flower manuals, one is amazed at the variety, the quaintness, the ingenuity, the charm, the technical handling (Figs. 1, 94) of bronze and clay, the perfection of whatever decorative detail (Figs. 51, 148) there is, and its subordination to the form; the almost lack of duplication, and the absolute faultlessness of design (Fig. 54) in the containers used in Japanese flower arrangement. Because of their beauty, a stream of them has flowed out like a river from Japan to the rest of the world.

Part of the reason for lack of duplication of fine containers was the fertility of invention and love of this art in the craftsmen themselves. No artist artisan from the 14th century on could see any good reason to duplicate a design when his imagination was bursting with ideas for others. Another reason was that each *daimyo* or feudal lord had among his retainers a bronze caster whose duty it was to design and cast whatever bronze articles the *daimyo* or his household needed, as expertly and beautifully as possible.

In Japan, the perception of beauty was not limited to a few at any time in the history of the nation, and some of those bronze casters had facile fingers which could translate their visions into enduring beauty. The result has been that some of their exquisite conceptions have been used by one generation after another. Today the proud possessor of one of those old bronze flower containers is thrilled by its enduring charm, to which no photograph can do entire justice. No one who possesses such a treasure ever grudges whatever money was put into its purchase because money cannot buy the inspiration which constantly emanates from such a container.

The householder, who had to buy containers, paid just as much, and sometimes perhaps a little more than he could afford. Flower containers are expensive but very necessary articles in a Japanese home. They were expected to be handed down as heirlooms; they were part of the wedding outfit and given as wedding presents and had as much consideration in the wedding outfit as many things we might consider vastly more important.

When these treasures were not in use they were stored in the godown, the fireproof storehouse, among the other family treasures. The fine old containers of the schools of floral art or of any skilled flower master, even the bamboo holders, were as reverently regarded as if they retained some of the artistic and spiritual power of their former owners, the floral masters, whose potency was thus carried over from one generation to another.

The constant and unvarying interest in flower arrangement in Japan from the 12th century until today gave the vase makers an ever-growing impetus which had its peak in the 17th century. There were endless varieties of the standard forms of erect, basin, and suspended shapes. It was important to every floral artist and school to have as wide an assortment of fine containers as possible so that the floral master or student was not hampered in the erection of a floral composition. It was "news" in the floral world when an entirely new floral style of composition was created. Many different forms of containers for flowers gave each designer freedom. The dull sameness of many American flower containers, turned out in a manufactory by the thousand, has tended to develop a sameness in American bouquets because it is easier to arrange flowers in the same way that every one else does.

In Japan when a man purchased a flower container for his use it was a matter of considerable importance. Would it suit the kind of flowers he commonly used? Would this or that container be the better? Was it the right height? Should it be bronze or pottery? Or did this one have the right width and size of bowl for the variety of iris the Japanese had in such quantity? All these questions and many more were of more importance than the price. These questions and problems are just as important in America today as they were in Japan two or three centuries ago. They are more difficult here in America today than they ever were in Japan, for lack of an established floral art, and the lack of an appreciation of the importance of the container in making a unit of design with the flower material.

In large cities in America one can find these lovely old containers without which people who are desirous of making Japanese flower arrangements feel nothing can be done. However, one can use the straight, dark green, cylindrical pottery containers often seen. Our early American potters made beautiful, richly colored jars which our grandmothers put pickles in. These can be used if one inserts a tin tube (not a galvanized iron one because it secretes a chemical injurious to the long life of cuttings) as suggested in the chapter on equipment. The arrangement can be made in the tube and the tube can then be inserted in the pickle jar. There is a distinct need for simple, dark, beautifully designed flower containers here in America.

Ashikaga Yoshimasa (*circa* 1436–1490) the most luxurious as well as the most art-loving sovereign Japan ever had, solved the idea of simplicity in flower containers in a very simple way by instituting the use of lengths of bamboo. In time we may be able to grow the right variety, the giant timber bamboo, *Phyllostachys reticulata* (*P. bambusoides*), or the short jointed one, the *P. edulis,* in quantities, but as yet it is impossible.

In Japan, the bamboo container (Figs. 4, 26, 29, 35, 38, 69, 71, 86) is indispensable to the floral artist. Its simplicity and adaption to the most formal as well as to the informal is conclusive proof that a plain, neutral color is the best for a flower container because the aim in this floral art is to make a finished work of art in all its aspects even though the most impermanent materials are used. The apparent natural casualness of this style of arrangement is very deceptive because every leaf, every part of a stem, every angle, every curve, every flower, in fact every single detail has been subjected to a rigid discrimination. The right container is a large part of the basic design.

Common sense was also an important part in flower containers which had wide mouths in order to admit air freely. (Fig. 71) Leaves were not permitted to touch the water even in basin forms for they quickly fouled the water. In large-mouthed containers the bamboo tube holding the stems was not visible above the water, but its use enabled the arrangement to rise from the center of the container with grace and strength without any visible support. The few stems were not crowded. They had air and deep water. (Fig. 77)

Aside from the common-sense ideas in flower containers, their simplicity and beauty, there was the question of rightness and charm for both the season and the material. The flower master, living and working with flower arrangement year after year, had a finely developed consciousness of association and suggestiveness, the fitting arrangement for the time and season. For instance, on a very hot day in summer when the sight and thought of a large expanse of water is cooling and refreshing, a traditional arrangement would be made of water plants, or those growing near the water, in as large a flower basin as possible; the water made part of the picture. In the winter, arrangements are made in erect containers in which the water is seen but is not played up as it is in the summer arrangements. (Fig. 25)

49

Many of the bronze basins have traditional designs engraved upon them which have a symbolic meaning. The stork and pine are both symbolical of long life and are often found on containers; maple trees are supposed to keep off noxious vapors; there are many containers poised on the crest of a wave that are delightful to hold water plants and are suggestive of banks of rivers or lakes. Baskets so much used in summer have many obvious meanings.

The correct mating of flower material and containers (Fig. 51) takes time to master, but it develops the imagination and has real importance. (Figs. 68, 85, 93, 96)

A checkup on the old floral manuals gives a few of the outstanding values. First comes the similarity between the flare of the container and the flare of the main stem. (Figs. 24, 70) Arrangement after arrangement shows that the curve or bend of the main stem corresponded to the main curve of the container. Occasionally when the leaves of the flower material were extremely pointed, the arrangement was made in a diamond-shaped basin (Fig. 51) and the whole effect was sharply triangular. The roundness of a peony blossom and the roundness of its bush were emphasized by putting the arrangement in a round basket (Fig. 108) or in a wide, round, bowl-shaped container with a short neck.

A very formal iris arrangement in a tall, straight bamboo emphasized the erectness of the tall blades by the straight sides of the container. (Fig. 26) Occasionally small leaves or blossoms (Fig. 51) pick up the same idea in the small inconspicuous blossoms decorating the container; or there may be a similarity in curve. Over and over again we see how the outstanding characteristics of material and container reciprocate each other in order to increase the value of both and emphasize the line effect. Many times the similarities and harmonies are subtle (Fig. 4) but once one achieves the understanding of a satisfying effect the result is positively thrilling.

The right container was thought to have a pivotal effect not only on the arrangement as a part of the design, but on the whole room. That is the reason why a floral artist would not make the first move, even in

50

thought, of an arrangement until he had satisfied himself as to the rightness of the container. The indecision over the choice of the right dress for an important occasion is not to be compared with the critical care with which the right container for the material on hand, for the occasion, and the season, was selected by the floral artist.

This decision was not made in the kitchen, or the flower room, but directly in front of the *tokonoma,* the place of honor where the arrangement was to be placed. They made no mistake. Japanese rooms are beautifully neutral in color, so it was not a matter of color but the rightness of the shape alone that was demanded. This, only, could make a unit of design in a flower arrangement in the *tokonoma* the center of interest of the entire room.

Chapter V

Line

Japanese floral art is like every other organized art in that each composition is a design built on related lines. Each line in a Japanese flower arrangement is clearly seen; each line is related to every other line and cannot be dispensed with without detriment to the whole composition. While each line is not a key line, it has its own important relationship in the arrangement as a whole.

Line in flower arrangement is just what it is everywhere, the path along which the eye travels from one point to another. This path or line, which should be as clearly seen in a flower arrangement as in a pictorial design, may be enhanced or adorned with flowers, just as an arabesque may be adorned with rosettes; the tips of the lines (or stems) may end in a flower or flowers, but wherever flowers are used in a Japanese flower arrangement they are used for color, contrast, and variety, and to present all the aspects of growing plant. Blossoms in themselves cannot *create* a line, but they can decorate it.

The stems *alone* of a plant, or the branches of a tree or shrub, make the lines in a Japanese flower arrangement. They alone are the structural basis of any flower composition just as lines are the structural basis of any pattern or pictorial design, sculptural form or effective piece of machinery. The leaves on a stem may be regarded as the shading of the line (Figs. 4, 54) or a projection of points along the line (Figs. 54, 82) calling attention to, or emphasizing the path the eye travels.

The aim of every artist of pictorial design or sculptor is to catch and "fix" the moment of "arrested motion." The floral artist aims to present the "moment of arrested growth in the life of a living plant" just as clearly as the candid camera aims to "catch the man in the act." The Japanese floral artist of the classic form of *Ikebana* uses his stems or

Fig. 52

This arrangement is built
on three lines closely united at the base. The
flowers and leaves are
"ornaments" of the design
and 'accents" of the line.

Fig. 53
Basic design of Fig. 52.

53

Fig. 54

Masses of flowers and leaves thicken and hide the lines but even
though the skeleton is clothed one senses the three related lines
that are the basis of the design.

54

branches as lines in order to project the personality of an idealized living plant in an apparently artless and unrestrained manner. We are not so conscious when we make floral compositions of the necessity of showing movement or action, because we are so unconscious of plant motion, the inner movements of growth. Yet even in unthinking moments we are cognizant that there is a vital difference between the "cut" flowers and the uncut.

The floral artist therefore attempts to restore the appearance of vitality or inner movement. His aim is to "put over" the moment of arrested motion in a flower arrangement by infusing the same feeling of vitality into "cut" stems as there is in uncut stems (Figs. 26, 69). This infusion of life can be done only by the use of line; that is, by using the stems or branches as an artist uses lines. He uses color (blooms) to enhance the beauty of the lines of a composition but they cannot impart vitality to a composition any more than masses of material can impart vitality. Vitality in a floral composition is obtained by the same means as vitality is obtained in a pictorial design, and that is by the radiating principle of lines (stems).

When a Japanese floral artist sees a cutting, when he selects his material, his eye takes in first the line of the stem. His mind then sweeps over his repertoire of patterns, and he mentally selects a pattern where the cutting fits in already or can be made to fit in.

The flower or flowers which may be on the cutting do not attract his attention except as subordinate to the line which can project the personality of the plant from which the cutting was taken. The flower is part of that personality. The artist looks over his material most carefully for the cutting that can make the main line of a pattern. The other lines can be more easily found. All cuttings have differing characteristics, beside varying from an almost straight stem to those with a great deal of curve.

As has been said, the use of any line in a Japanese floral composition is not a casual one. Though a floral composition has one main line, each line in a composition has a relationship to this main line *and* to every

55

Fig. 55

Only a floral artist of a hundred or more years ago would or could have made this arrangement of 999 stems of rice willow, and placed an *ashirai* of a branch of *nanten* berries in a *keikwa*. It had to be a large arrangement, for each stem had its own place in the whole—yet how suggestive of early spring with the late winter *nanten* berries! Those old floral artists liked to hitch these two seasons together, almost as if they hated to see winter go as much as they liked to see spring come. Artistically and artificially this is a truly marvelous landscape arrangement. There is indescribable grace in the three main lines.

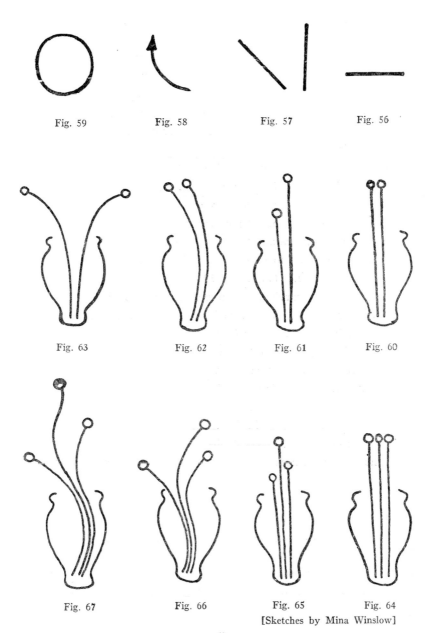

Fig. 59   Fig. 58   Fig. 57   Fig. 56

Fig. 63   Fig. 62   Fig. 61   Fig. 60

Fig. 67   Fig. 66   Fig. 65   Fig. 64

[Sketches by Mina Winslow]

other line in the composition, whether it is a 1000-stem rice willow or one of the popular three-line arrangements. If it is one line in the 1000 (strictly 999) stem arrangement, it has its own place in one of three groups and cannot be left out without making a hole or break in the composition. Needless to say what happens to a three-line composition if one line is lacking. Each line, in any Japanese flower arrangement, has its own particular function. It cannot be left out nor can another line be added without ruining the composition.

It is an axiom in pictorial design that any straight line, whether it is vertical or horizontal, is static, a line at rest; it does nothing, it goes nowhere, it says nothing. Even an oblique or slanting line does not give much sense of motion, but a curved ascending line has a strong sense of urge to go somewhere and to keep on going, no matter where the line ends. If it is allowed to go on, ideally it ends in a circle followed by another *ad infinitum*. (Figs. 58, 59) One rarely finds one branch, whether straight or curving, that possesses enough in itself to make an interesting composition. However Figure 105 illustrates such a one.

Two straight lines or stems (Figs. 56, 57) whether of the same length or different lengths have no point of interest unless there is a flower or flowers on the ends that catch the eye, because the sense of independence is so pronounced. There is no relationship; on the contrary they actually repel each other. Therefore, there can be no design. Put two ascending curved stems in a container in the same way and though there is a little more feeling of interest, especially if they are of different lengths, there is still no line design because of the same repulsion. There is however an emphatic urge to go somewhere or do something, but even the curve of the stems does not remove—it even emphasizes—this repulsion (Fig. 63).

If there are three straight stems, there is companionship but still no relationship and it is easy to see that there can be only increasing confusion without relationship, no matter how many more stems are inserted in the container. Mass, or number, in itself does not make line designs or line patterns, and if there is no relationship of lines there is no vitality. Such a mass or number of stems depends entirely upon color for interest.

Fig. 69

The "arrangement" in this illustration seems very slight but it is a good projection of personality.

Fig. 68

How statuesque, and yet how freely the lines of the chrysanthemum stems rise!

Fig. 70

The lines of the material and the lines of the container make a perfect unit of design.

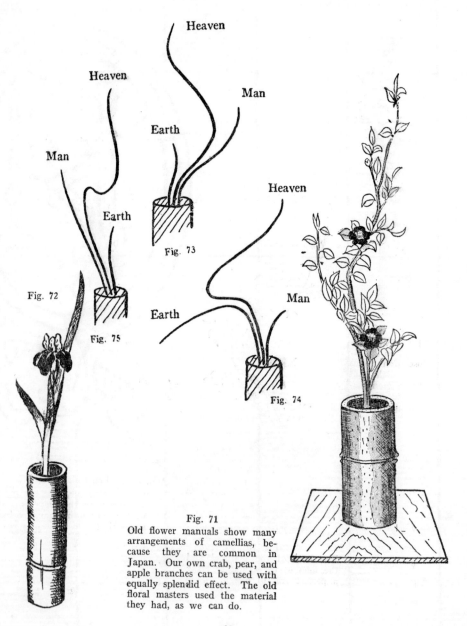

Heaven

Heaven

Man

Earth

Man

Earth

Fig. 72

Fig. 73

Fig. 75

Heaven

Earth

Man

Fig. 74

Fig. 71
Old flower manuals show many
arrangements of camellias, because they are common in
Japan. Our own crab, pear, and
apple branches can be used with
equally splendid effect. The old
floral masters used the material
they had, as we can do.

60

The aims are still all "cut" stems, non-vital. While the difference in the length of the stems and the color of the flowers may make the bouquet attractive, color and length of stems do not make a floral composition of line because line implies relationship among the parts and has nothing to do with color, however much color may add to the attractiveness of line designs (Fig. 70).

But, if three ascending curved stems are used, whether they are all the same length or not, the feeling of motion, or a sense of urge is strong, more emphatically so if they are of different lengths. If they are joined at the base closely for several inches, it is curious what vitality at once appears. This close union of the stems at the base, especially if it is for a length of several inches, has done three things: it has infused life into lifeless stems; it has made a floral pattern, a design; and it presents a moment of arrested growth. This radiation of lines from a seen or known point is the secret of vitality in all graphic art (Figs. 69, 71).

One of the first things that strikes one in these lines is the necessity for cutting the stems long enough to make a pattern. It is evident, too, that since the container and material make one unit of design, there must be a relationship between these two as well as between the floral lines. It is also obvious that the plant material ought to have distinction and style in order to make an arrangement of nice discrimination.

From the illustrations it is plain that three floral lines are enough to satisfy a feeling for mass, for height, for design, for movement, and for interest, if the lines are right—if the lengths of the three lines are well proportioned, and if the spaces between the lines are correct (though the spacing depends on the lines, and their angles with each other)—and all this depends to a great extent on long stems.

An odd number of lines adds vitality and charm impossible to attain with an even number of floral lines. In an arrangement of more than five lines the eye may become confused unless the floral design has been done with distinguished skill and taste. Three lines is a popular number for a flower arrangement because, if it is well proportioned, they are enough for any room.

61

Fig. 76

A plum arrangement that has style and vitality in its lines. It is triangular and tridimensional. Its flowers beautifully decorate the stem in a natural way. The basket arrangement shows that it is a late plum. The *nemoto* is well proportioned. The arrangement rises with vigor from the center of the container. The tip of the heaven stem is well over the point where the stems emerge from the water; the angles are sharp; the spaces balanced. It is about three and one fourth times the height of the container.

62

The predominating line must show style, strength, and a vital energy, as well as a subtle alliance with the line of the container. It must be able to say something (Fig. 70). All the lines of a Japanese flower arrangement must sweep into the lines and proportion of the room they are designed for, but in a three-line arrangement the predominating line must surpass the other two in strength of curve, in length, and in beauty. It is surprising how a comparatively slight change in the main line affects the whole design; it may enchance the effect or may cause it to lose its snap. This main line is commonly called the "heaven" line.

The other two lines, called the "man" line and the "earth" line, must present a contrast not only to the heaven line but to each other. No two lines in a Japanese flower arrangement may ever be the same length or may ever cross each other. In an erect arrangement (Fig. 76) the man line is the secondary one. The heaven and the man lines together determine the style of the arrangement (Fig. 71) while the earth line completes and balances the design. The heaven line clearly shows the plant personality, erect, drooping (Fig. 97), its character and growth. A branch of plum cannot possible take the smoothly flowing, graceful droop of a branch of forsythia or willow (Fig. 83).

The illustrations give some idea of a few of the traditional designs and how the second and third lines (stems) are affected; their directions, curves, and relationships to the main line of heaven. The angles the stems make at the point of division must be strong and full of contrast (Fig. 71) or they will destroy an otherwise beautiful arrangement.

The length of the secondary lines, the man and earth, may vary from almost one extreme to the other *if* kept in harmony and balance with each other with the heaven line. These lines, man and earth, are never under any circumstances of equal length or of the length of the heaven line. The usual proportions make the man line about two thirds the length of the heaven line and the earth line about one third the length of the heaven line. The actual height of the heaven line depends on the material used. If tree branches are used, the height may be four even five times the height of the container (Figs. 2, 26, 37) *if* it is an erect

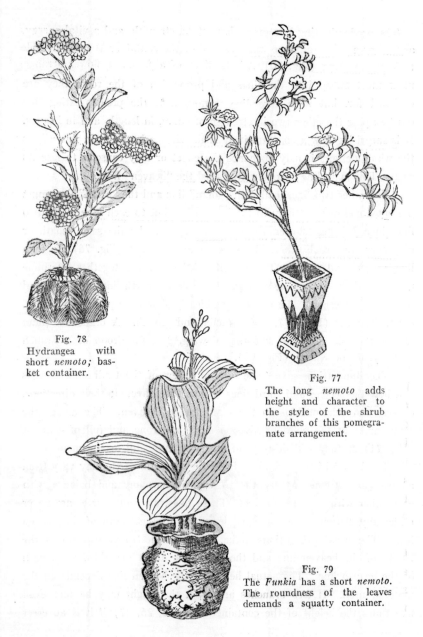

Fig. 78
Hydrangea with short *nemoto;* basket container.

Fig. 77
The long *nemoto* adds height and character to the style of the shrub branches of this pomegranate arrangement.

Fig. 79
The *Funkia* has a short *nemoto.* The roundness of the leaves demands a squatty container.

one. In a basin container the height may be considerably less and much more branching (Figs. 44, 94). Again, the height of the room and the height of the container and its style have an influence.

The height of a Japanese flower arrangement should *never be less than once and a half the height of an erect container, or once and a half the greatest width of a basin container*. Height, which is so necessary for elegance and style, is dependent on the character of the material, its flexibility, and length, and its adaptability, as well as the height of the room in which it is to be placed. An arrangement of three stems of tree branches can be of considerable height because they sweep into the lines of a room so grandly.

The length of the close union of stems between the waterline and the point of diversion (this length is called the *nemoto*) is a matter of adjustment according to the season of the year and the material. The *nemoto* is shorter in the summer than in the winter. Tree branches naturally have a longer *nemoto* than flower stems. This close union of stems is important because it gives great strength to all the lines, cements the relationship of lines, and gives vitality. The *nemoto* gives the same vitality to a flower arrangement that is given by the trunk of a tree, springing with a great impetus from the earth uncluttered by any growth at its base. If the *nemoto* is well done it gives the same sense of stability that the roots of a tree give. The stems give the impression of keeping this close union clear to the bottom of the container and of being firmly fastened there even though the arrangement may seem in some instances to be considerably off center (Fig. 80). The tip of the heaven stem should be almost or quite directly over the point where the stems emerge from the water. This also adds to the vitality, because a proper sense of gravity is felt.

The three ascending curved stems, heaven, man, earth, because of their harmonious flow of curves with no crossing of lines, start a rhythm, a movement like the musical beat of 1–2–3. Movement aids greatly in sense and appearance of vitality. The rhythm has strength because of the strong line below the point of diversion of stems whence each line

65

Fig. 80

Though this arrangement is considerably off center it has weight enough to be not unpleasing. Such a balance is often seen in nature.

Fig. 81

Here the floral artist increased the value of the arrangement by skilful cutting. The Ikebana shows balance and flowing rhythm, proportion and height, and a certain sturdy, strength.

or stem takes its own free, unconfused path (Fig. 76). It is surprising what a variety of patterns can result from three lines which differ in direction, in length and in curve, radiating in easy fluency from the point of diversion—floral designs that spring from the center of the container without any visible support, designs whose lines begin with the container, flow out from it and yet are contained within its limits. Each design presents itself as a single complete unit with a vital rhythm. As a result many Japanese flower arrangements look more alive and more beautiful than many living plants (Fig. 54).

The stems are so placed in the center of the container that the design is triangular and tridimensional in form. The leaves give depth to the form and aid in the modeling; the flowers (if there are any) are the "ornaments of design" and add the color, contrast, and variety necessary to make the arrangement present a highly idealized plant personality. The result is a flower arrangement that is a superbly posed plant individuality of dynamic and vital charm (Fig. 82).

The old flower philosophers in order to fix firmly in the mind of the student the fact that line relationship was important in a flower composition, and perhaps to link up the floral art to the world we live in, named the three lines, using the Chinese terms, *shin, soe, tai,* or the Japanese *ten-jin-chi,* as we say "heaven, man, earth"; some schools (in order to be individual) call them "father, mother, child," or "sun, moon, earth," or any cosmic unity.

All these cosmic unities are eternally linked together, three varying elements, each element widely different from the others, each necessary to the other, each independent but an indispensable part of a perfect whole. It shows in a very simple way how much a part of the Japanese people flower arrangement grew to be, a part of the structure of living and being, a link as it were between the universe and man.

Chapter VI

Patterns

To the uninitiated, the thought of using definite patterns for making a flower arrangement may seem utterly absurd, yet nature herself does this. Each plant, each tree, has its own pattern for stem, leaf, and flower and follows the pattern quite consistently if left to itself. Man has learned that every art has its own standards, basic patterns on which he builds variations or makes new designs.

In Japan, the floral patterns on which Japanese flower arrangements are built are easily recognizable as many variations of the triangle. These triangle line designs have many variations of the traditional patterns, which have naturally evolved because of the variance in plant life, and the gradual development of the art, but the basic design is always clear. As the preceding chapter on line has shown, the lines in a good flower composition are few, simple, and unconfused from beginning to end. They start from a close union of stems (lines) and each line then flows freely and apparently unrestrainedly so that the eye cannot become confused and lose the design.

Can stems and branches be made into patterns and can all plant material be fitted into a pattern so that the stems may be made into an arrangement that follows the paper pattern? The chapter on line shows how each stem becomes a line, an extremely important line, fulfilling its own definite function. It follows that the very short-stemmed plants are not often usable, nor are stems that are too soft to stand upright and assume direction. (This does not exclude vines, which have their own rules.) A stem must be firm enough to become a line; it must be firm enough to maintain itself in an erect position or, if necessary, to be bent, and it must stand up a reasonable length of time after arrangement. All these qualities are needed to make that subtle alliance with the container,

Fig. 82

Three stems of a lily make a delightful arrangement, each stem acting as a line in a variation of the pattern shown in Figure 87. The leaves are all in good condition; the *nemoto* shows late summer. The drum-shaped container is very suggestive to me of placees abounding in large round rocks where I have picked these lilies. The flowers are well placed and have been picked with the idea of having the pleasure of seeing the buds open.

69

to make unit of design.

The problem, therefore, of adapting a stem to a line pattern is a new one for each material and resolves itself into reducing to a common denominator the obvious points of the plant material—the length of stems, their flexibility and firmness, the character and position of the leaves. Leaves add grace and charm to the lines of a pattern in a Japanese arrangement, and should be as perfect as possible. They add emphasis to the personality of the stem or branch used and they are an actual aid to the vitality of life and line.

The fact that living material has to be dealt with complicates the problem of floral design because the pattern has to be viewed from the standpoint of actual vitality as well as the appearance of vitality. Nothing but close observance of nature and acquaintance with growing plants can give the student of floral design the right hypothesis between design and living form because this matter of design and pattern is not that of conventionalizing a flower form but of correctly simulating an *ideal* living plant, and also expressing its inner spiritual quality. One who has cultivated a garden and who loves trees with all their individual differences has a good background for selection and appreciation of the floral patterns used in Japanese flower arrangement.

Every pattern consists of three lines of varying lengths and directions. The heaven line may vary from an almost perpendicular, as in Figure 87, to a line whose curvature is strongly bent back laterally from a point just above the point of diversion, then curved sharply back so as to bring the tip of the line almost or quite directly above the place where the stems emerge from the water, thus establishing a center of gravity. It is important that this center of gravity be established in each arrangement.

In the different shiftings of the three lines of a floral design, the heaven line may show all sorts of variations between the two extremes—almost perpendicular and very deeply bowed—but as the heaven line varies so must the man and earth lines vary (Fig. 91) in order to maintain a consistent harmony of contrast and balance (Figs. 88, 89, 92). The illustrations show these extremes and offer practical examples of the adap-

70

Fig. 84

A variation of the pattern shown in Figure 87, one of the most popular because of its simplicity. The plum and magnolia make a felicitous spring arrangement in a bronze engraved with wild geese and waves.

Fig. 83

A March wind arrangement in a fish basket container. The willow branches have a *nejime* of button chrysanthemums. This pattern is shown in Figure 91 with variations.

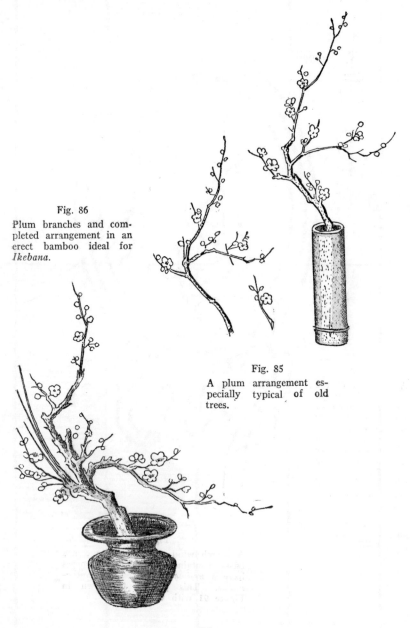

Fig. 86
Plum branches and completed arrangement in an erect bamboo ideal for *Ikebana*.

Fig. 85
A plum arrangement especially typical of old trees.

72

tions of materials to patterns, since one often finds branches bent in all these ways; they also show how the same material (Figs. 50, 76, 86, 95) may be used in different designs and still be correct. The type patterns have been numbered for convenient reference.

The lengths of stems, cut into the properly proportioned heaven, man, earth, must assume vitality, unite in a pattern that is characteristic of the material, and take on style. Therefore these patterns must be simple and natural, so that the *ikebana* may seem simple and natural. The artist must know his pattern-designs so well that the instant he takes a stem in his hand some one of several may leap into his mind and he can choose a pattern that will suit his material before it wilts.

Before the arranger can decide on his pattern, he must look over his stock of containers. The height of a container or its width, in a basin container, is important as I have said before, because the material and container are to make a unit of design. A basin container too must not be too deep, or it will tend to choke a design (Fig. 98). Unless the height of an arrangement is *at least once and a half* the height of the container, the heaven line will seem cramped and topless even though the proportions are good. (Fig. 98) An arrangement must be tall enough so that the tips of the branches will not seem to end but to flow off until they seem to vanish into space.

It is well to remember to keep firmly in mind that it is important to show a fine balance and proportion between the heaven branch and the other two branches and again between the man and earth branches. A consistent proportion (Figs. 76, 85, 101) and balance of length should always be maintained among all the branches, a difficult thing for a student to do until his sense of proportion has been trained. The curves must also have beautifully balanced contrasts, and the angles made by the stems at the point of diversion must be strong and well balanced. The variance in plant material even in the same species is such that there can be many variations of these line patterns as the illustrations show.

A checkup of many old flower manuals shows that every phase of branch form may be seen in most tree forms, i.e., erect, drooping, slanting,

73

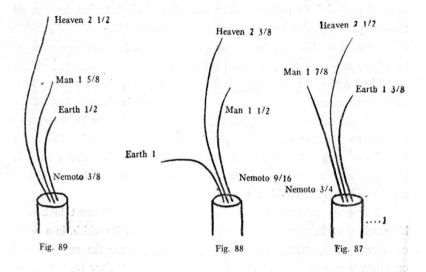

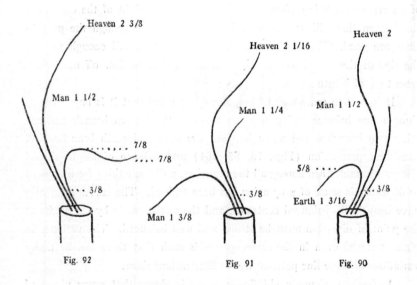

Japanese Floral Patterns

Fig. 94

How lovely is this flow of line in the plum arrangement in the low container. The long *nemoto,* the low branch as if hanging over the water, the sharp angles of each of the man and earth lines with the heaven line, all unite in an arrangement having restraint, balance, vitality, rhythm, and the certain elegance that comes only from height. Pattern variation of Figure 91.

Fig. 93

It is hard to believe there are seven branches in this arrangement of pine, which follows so closely its characteristic habit. The *usubata* used for the container and the flare of the main stem are good. The basic lines are those of the pattern shown in Figure 87.

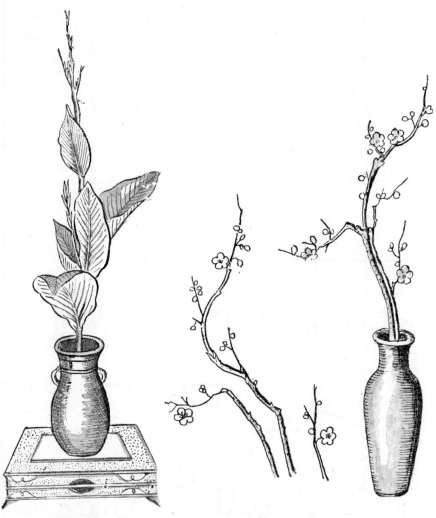

Fig. 96

A stately variation of the pattern shown in Figure 87, showing how the man or earth line can be shortened. Our familiar canna shows how interesting five large leaves and two flower stems can be.

Fig. 95

These three stems of plum are used for the lines of the pattern in Figure 88. As in many cases there is little bending or straightening needed if the right pattern is selected.

so that these patterns, as well as many other typical forms may be seen to represent truthfully a natural branch of most kinds of trees even though the tree forms vary; a pine is not like a maple. (Figs. 41, 47) Part of this difference is in the foliage and part in the angle that the branches make with the trunk. These angles should be accurately represented, if possible, in the angles made by the stems at the point of diversion. Those plants or trees having great vertical straightness (Fig.52) can be adapted to the pattern shown in Figure 87 while the other patterns go gradually through the widely varying slants or curves (all found in nature) used in Japanese flower arrangement.

The *nemoto* varies from two to six inches dependent on the material and the time of the year. The average length is about four inches. The flower materials that are used the year round (Figs. 26, 83, 104). especially the two season materials, make the *nemoto*, in Japan, an important feature. It helps in showing the season of the year and it gives strength and character to an arrangement; it emphasizes the simplicity and the triangular, tridimensional style of an arrangement. It makes each design easy to see and aids in clarifying each line.

The *nemoto* also aids in the feeling that each flower is an "ornament of design"! The treatment of flowering stems is little different from the treatment of leafy stems without flowers because each bloom in a Japanese flower arrangement is considered as a formally placed ornament. Flowers must not overload a stem; they must adorn it. If the blooms are small, more blooms can be used but *all* blooms are used with great discretion. It will be interesting for the reader to check over the illustrations in the book just for this point, to see how many ways blooms are used. Only practice can teach the student that one pattern is better for a given material than another, for the triple harmony of material and its personality, container and its harmonious relation to material and the pattern and its place in the unit of design.

The most valuable material for practice in making patterns is the red osier, common in the middle west at least all the year around; long stems of privet or pussy willow are also good material and common. Constant

77

Fig. 98
A simple arrangement of *Poly-gonum* showing triangular effect.

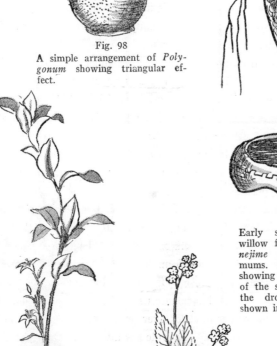

Fig. 97
Early spring arrangement of willow for a felicitous occasion *nejime* of button chrysanthemums. A superb use of willow showing how the upward thrust of the strong trunk counteracts the drooping twigs. Pattern shown in Fgiure 92.

Fig. 100
Most striking contrast to the *Polygonum* above. Pattern shown in Figure 89.

Fig. 99
Primula without *nemoto;* variation of pattern shown in figure 89.

78

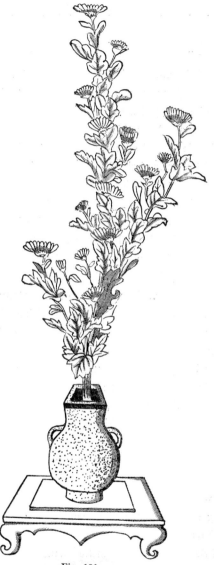

Fig. 101

An arrangement of chrysanthemums which shows clearly how flowers are used as "ornaments of design." They are plainly subordinate to the line design yet they aid greatly in the vitality of this living art. The pattern stands out plainly triangular and tridimensional.

79

practice with these long, easily bended stems is invaluable in order to learn how to follow a line, to make patterns, to practice bending, to get the "feeling of line," and saves using more valuable or more expensive material. This practice is learning to draw with living lines.

In May or June, even earlier according to location, flowering fruit branches can be arranged with much greater success after long practice with these other stems. After this exacting training, one clearly comprehends why great double blooms are never allowed in *Ikebana*. Japanese floral art is too refined to overload slender stems with heavy spots of color.

There are many slender flowering stems such as flowering almond, snapdragon, unbranching delphinium, *Dictamus*, that are delightful to use for simple line arrangements. These can also be used with a heaven line of evergreen or other leafy branches . Practice with flowering stems and green stems gives the student the added pleasure of using color. It also lessens the expense of flowers, which can be used with seasonal and regional green branches, gives variety, and lessens monotony in flower arrangement.

All the details that go into the composition of a floral arrangement— selection of material and container, proportion of height and pattern—all must be thought out before making a Japanese flower arrangement.

Nothing but practice, constant drill with actual stems, all kinds of stems, will give the necessary training and skill needed in *Ikebena*. Charts may be made of these patterns that are illustrated, and hung up so as to keep before the student the ideal while he is building an arrangement, but there is no easy short cut to fine eye training in exactness; that must be learned by constant comparison of arrangement and pattern.

If possible keep the arrangement against a plain background to compare it with the chart. The eye can then pick out each fault so much more clearly and easily than one can when the arrangement is against a figured background.

One of the most delightful of the results of this eye-training is found in the pleasure gained in seeing these patterns in every tree and shrub met on a walk in street or garden. Nature suddenly seems to come alive and talk in a familiar way of her secrets.

Chapter VII

Preparation of Material and Bending of Stems

The preparation of the material for a flower arrangement is an important detail of any arrangement of flowers. It is particularly so of a Japanese flower arrangement, whose every detail has been so expertly systematized. The Japanese have many so-called *hi-den* (secrets) concerning preservatives, as well as many simple, common-sense ideas, such as the cutting of the stems under water, and bruising, or burning, or boiling the ends of stems, which are gradually becoming well known. Many of the *hi-den* are useless to print, either because the materials take too much time in preparation, or are hard to get and so would not be used. The notes appended on the care and preservation of cuttings are from different sources and have been tried repeatedly; they apply to cuttings in general, are simple, and commonly successful.

Material from the florist's does not need extra attention because a good florist has done all he can to preserve his material. However, even so, it is merely a matter of precaution to "harden" it in deep water for an hour so that the material can adjust itself to a different temperature. If one has to depend on florist material go to a grower, or if possible a wholesale dealer, and tell him the kind of material you will want from time to time. If you must depend on a retail dealer let him know you want freshly delivered material, long stems, and leaves plentiful and in good condition. Flowers should never be allowed to stand in a draft. When flowers wilt it means they are not sucking up enough water, or have not been hardened, are too warm or in a draft.

Flower material from the garden or from anywhere outdoors is best gathered in the evening about sundown, early in the morning, or on cloudy or wet days, *not* in the bright hot sun or wind. A sharp knife which makes a long slanting cut is much better than dull scissors which cut straight across the stem. The stems must be cut longer than the arrangement has been planned for, so as to give freedom in using them and to allow for possible bending. It is better to cut most flowers but dahlias in bud, because the arrangement lasts longer and gives the added pleasure of seeing the buds open. All leaves should be removed from the lower four inches of the stems.

As soon as the material can be rushed into the house plunge each stem into water and cut off an inch of stem *under* the water so that the water can rush up into the stem before the air enters the stems. The slanting cut allows more water to enter the stems. Most woody stems such as chrysanthemums, tree branches and flowering shrubs absorb water freely if their stems for an inch or two are well crushed. Large blooms, such as single peonies, chrysanthemums, or dahlias (the use of the word "large" is a comparative one, because really large blooms are not used in *Ikebana*) may be wrapped in wet cloths during all the preliminary care of the cuttings. These blooms (picked in the bud with the exception of dahlias) should be regulated to the size of the design so that a line is not overloaded.

All milky-stemmed blooms should have their stems burned as soon as cut. Protect all but the part to be burned with wet cloths.

Hollow stemmed flowers should have their stems dipped into boiling water a few seconds, after the other parts have been protected.

Evergreens and very hardy tree branches should have their bark stripped for a couple of inches, the ends crushed, and in winter when the greens are dirty a bath in slightly warm soapy water with a clear water rinse and two days immersion in deep water makes them fresh and crisp. They are often enabled by this treament to lose the sun rusted appearance common in winter. An arrangement of evergreens often lasts three to six weeks. The long soaking makes the stems more pliant.

All garden flowers and tree and shrub branches should be stood in deep pails of water overnight in a dark, cool place if possible. By this treatment their stems fill with water and they are tempered to a different atmosphere; they become hardened and ready to arrange.

Many flowers, roses for example, which have begun to wilt can be restored to freshness by making a slanting cut off the ends and putting them into fairly hot water for an hour or until the water has become cool, then putting them into fresh cool water in a dark place for some hours.

Hydrangeas wilt very quickly. The best treatment for them is to crush the stems very quickly and then boil them in vinegar until the color changes. Follow with the deep cool water and allow them to rest overnight.

Plants with a slimy juice should be put into a saturated solution of alum for a few minutes.

The above rules take care of all ordinary stems with good results. Occasionally a plant will respond to one treatment more effectually than to another, but one has to find that out by experience.

Forsythia and flowering fruit branches are forced quickly and easily by putting the cuttings into a pail of hot water daily, until the buds show signs of opening. Keep them in the sunshine if possible.

Bending Stems and Branches

It is quite surprising that some slight bending of stems and branches is not more common in all kinds of flower arrangement because a slight bend below a bloom or leaf to make the stem appear a little more graceful and fluent may make the difference between a charming arrangement and one that lacks ease. A little pressure applied by wet fingers along the length of a stiff stem will limber it up most agreeably and attractively. The rigidity of the line is lessened but not the essential character.

There are few patterns in Japanese flower arrangement that do not show a pronounced curve. There are few stems in nature that do not show more or less curve. Some of the curves in *Ikebana* may be natural or they may have been induced; it should be impossible to tell which is which. The ease or difficulty with which these wanted curves are made naturally depends on the material. In the case of a great deal of plant material, bending of stem may not be needed at all if one knows his patterns well. Knowledge of stems is acquired by long practice and training in bending straight or nearly straight stems to copy patterns. The eye becomes

Fig. 102

The angular twist of this evergreen is greatly enhanced by the
nejime of chrysanthemums.

Fig. 103

This shows what a charming
arrangement can be made without any bending. It is *Begonia
Evansiana.* Note the long *nemoto.*

accustomed to recognize patterns and parts of patterns in plant life and to look everywhere for them, until finally plant material falls naturally into groups of usable patterns.

For actual practice in bending stems to form lines, select the easiest pattern (Fig. 87) and easy material such as red osier. This lovely red-stemmed shrub can be found growing in waste places winter and summer, and often also in garden plantings. In summer strip off all leaves and little branchlets of a stem about thirty inches long. Allow twelve inches for insertion in container and *nemoto*. The center of the curve for this branch is about twenty inches from the tip. Grasp the stem firmly at this point, put the two thumbs together, close together, on the inside of the curve-to-be and gently bend the stem with a force just short of breaking.

Keep the fingers wet and move the hands slowly, first towards one end of the curve-to-be towards the *nemoto*; then again grasp the center of the curve-to-be and repeat the process until within two inches of the tip. Repeat the whole process until the bend is satisfactory. Practice with the pattern in front of you and practice every line of every pattern until you feel confident that you know the process and can follow a pattern. Remember that this is not only a manual dexterity practice but it trains the eye as nothing else can.

When a fair amount of dexterity has been gained, do not strip the stems of leaves but learn to put the thumbs between the joints so that the leaves will not be bruised or torn off. The stem is much more brittle at the joints, therefore great care must be taken at those points not to break the stem. It is best to include within the grasp whatever leaves or small blooms there are on the stem; otherwise they may be broken off.

Sometimes, if just a slight curve is needed, it is enough to grasp the stem firmly with the left hand at the point where the *nemoto* would come, while the right hand slowly bends the stem with a heavy pressure of thumb and four fingers passing along the desired curve. If the stem is thick and woody, a series of small transverse cuts on the top of the stem makes it easier to bend; a twisting motion when bending also makes the stem more pliant. It is not possible for every stem to obtain an exaggerated curvature

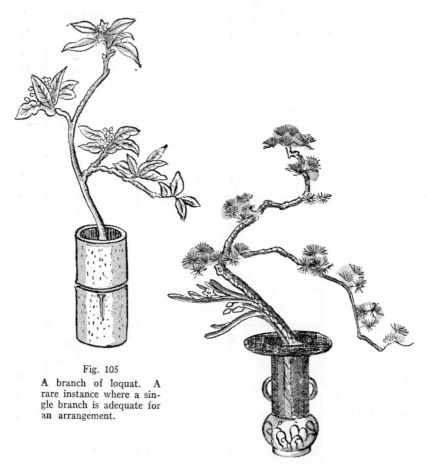

Fig. 105

A branch of loquat. A rare instance where a single branch is adequate for an arrangement.

Fig. 104

A superb posing of this branch of pine, with its suggestion of home on a wind-tortured hillside, and its lovely *nejime* of narcissus. Angularity can be as eye-filling as curves.

Careful selection of branches with something of the curve desired is the wise way to go about making an *ikebana*.

When a branch is very refractory, dip a cloth in hot vinegar and bind it tightly around the spot to be most bent (taking care that the leaves are pushed aside and protected). It will soften the fibres enough so that the heated, bent stem will not spring back if the stem is at once put under the coldwater tap or immersed, still bent, in cold water for some little time. During the time of immersion in cold water the bend must be tied in the shape desired.

Some evergreens, *Juniperus Pfitser* for instance, have good natural curves that need only to be exaggerated. One of these branches can be tied in a greater curve, immersed for twenty-four hours in cold water, arranged while still tied and kept tied until the branch is dry, before removing the tyings. It will then conform to the pattern desired. If the tips do not turn up at the ends, I wet my fingers in water nearly every time I pass the arrangement and coax them into keeping the charming upward tilt so much liked because it is a natural curve.

A bend may be induced by putting the point of curvature under the hot water tap. Hold the stem firmly with both hands (leaves pushed aside and protected) under the stream of hot water so that the heat and moisture can soften the stem while the hands slowly twist and bend it. Always take time to do bending slowly and gently, but firmly and persistently, as long as is necessary to make the desired curve. After five minutes or so (under the hot water tap) move the branch, still bent over, under the cold water tap until so chilled that the curve will not relapse. The curve should always be made a little more than desired because there will always be a slight spring back.

Bent branches are more used by the skilled floral artist than by the amateur, but the amateur may just as quickly add this bit of grace and charm to an arrangement of any kind as an artist adds it to the heaven, man and earth lines.

There are many materials of an angular nature, burr oak and its more feminine counterpart, the winged *Evonymus,* and the pine, as well as other

87

trees whose angularity is natural and is the charm of their own peculiar beauty. Emphasize this angularity not by bending but by choice of pattern. While the patterns, shown as patterns, are curved lines, the illustrations of arrangements show how the curves resolve themselves into more or less angularity (without any lessening of charm) according to the material used.

After all, the important point is the projection of the plant personality whether this is brought about by flowing curves or rigid angularity. Burr oak is a good example of rigid lines and yet there is no more fascinating material if it is arranged in the early spring when the little green tufts of velvety leaves make so great a contrast to the severe angularity of the ridged branches.

Chapter VIII

Yang and *Ying*, *In* and *Yo*
or
The Masculine and Feminine
in
Japanese Flower Arrangement

One cannot read any of the few books or the many magazine articles written on the subject of Japanese flower arrangement without coming upon the Chinese words *Yang* and *Ying* or the Japanese *In* and *Yo* or their loose English equivalents, masculine and feminine, or right and left, applied to this art. These phrases are all terms applied to the two great forces recognized in the Far East as the forces that regulate and are responsible for all life. To the ordinary person such terms applied to flower arrangement may seem far-fetched, even a matter of affectation, and out of place, and so they might be in American floral arrangements; but floral art in Japan grew with the people and made part of their lives. Thus the terms and the words of speech in common use were easily and naturally applied to flower arrangement.

To substitute others today in Japan would be impossible. We Americans, as a nation, are too young, or too old, to make use of the cosmic ideas that were common in Japan when this art began. There is no religion in Japanese flower arrangement, as many would have us believe, but it *is* saturated with cosmic ideas. Cosmic and religious ideas are utterly different and distinct.

Flower arrangements as manifested by the *shin-no-hana*, the altar arrangements, were an aid to religion. The cosmic terms, *Yang* and *Ying* or *In* and *Yo*, to keep the Japanese terms, were commonly used as terms of strong contrast, such as strong and weak, light and dark, right and left, and really meant little more; *but* when used by floral artists they accounted

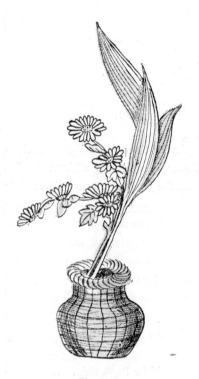

Fig. 107

A feminine arrangement
of *Aspidistra* leaves with
a *nejime* of chrysanthe-
mums.

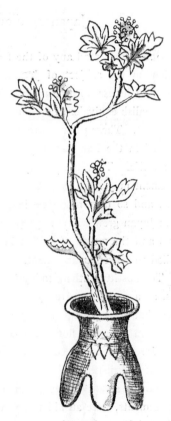

Fig. 106

A masculine arrangement
of *Aralia*.

90

for and applied the law of contrast, the balance of inequalities, prevented weak or monotonous arrangements, abolished symmetry, and in so doing created beauty.

According to cosmic ideas all the qualities of greatest vigor are *In* or masculine. Therefore a fully opened flower is masculine while a half-opened flower or bud is feminine; the strong colors—red, pink, purple, or variegated—are all masculine, and the yellow, blue, and white are feminine. The upper half of a leaf is masculine, the under half, feminine; a stem in itself is masculine or feminine according as the bow or curve faces the right or left.

When words of such strong contrast are so constantly used, it follows of necessity that one is alive to and makes use of the laws of contrast and balance. It also works in with the idea of using all the aspects of plant life, stem, leaf and flower, so that the result or aim of a flower arrangement—to produce a highly idealized living plant or as I have stated before "a moment of arrested growth in the life of a living plant"—was realized. It is hard for us to understand that if a *Yang* was present a *Ying* had to be, whether it related to blooms or part of the design, long and short branches, upper and under side of leaves. In short, the whole effect was a balanced one. The number of leaves was restricted so that each leaf could be seen to have its own place in the design. Not only that but some leaves must show the upper sides, others the lower, or show both sides (Fig. 108), while others are tilted to give a different but perfectly natural effect. If a flower arrangement is overloaded with either blooms or leaves, the sense of balance is lost and values and contrasts are overlooked until the design is not apparent.

The illustration (Fig. 108) of a peony arrangement shows many of the above-mentioned ideas very clearly. Peonies are difficult to arrange well because of the size of the blooms and the luxuriance of the leaves.

As an arrangement it is a masculine or right-hand arrangement (right or left as the arranger stands behind it). One fully opened bloom (masculine) is balanced by one half-open bloom (feminine) and one bud (also feminine). It is a single peony because large double blooms are too

Fig. 108

A masculine arrangement of a peony showing how the principles of *Yang*
and *Ying* or *In* and *Yo* are employed. A large flower is balanced by a bud
and a half-open bloom. The leaves have been thinned out so that the arrangement does not have too much bulk; a proportion of leaves show the upper
sides, some show the under, and others show parts of both sides. The arrangement presents a moment of "arrested growth" in the life of a living plant.
It has vitality, animation, restraint, rhythm, balance, unity, and contrast in an
admirable degree. It is a fine "unit of design."

heavy to use in a flower arrangement. The tall, main stem is balanced by the out-curving lateral stem and the short third stem opposite. The leaves have been thinned out so that each leaf may be clearly seen to occupy its own place in the design in a perfectly natural and pleasant way. The number of leaves is enough for mass and few enough for style and thoughtful disposition of each one.

The arrangement has height and breadth enough to show the plant habit. It is over three times the height of the basket container. As a unit of design it is perfect because the rounded form of the basket container picks up the flare of the heaven line, the roundness of the peony bush itself (the plant habit) and the blossom; yet the arrangement as a whole is triangular and tridimensional. It is full of vitality and yet it is simple and informal as suits an early summer arrangement, and yet full enough to suggest the luxuriance of summer. It is easy to see the perfection of every detail—the length of the *nemoto*, freely rising from the center without any visible support; the strong angles at the point of diversion; well-balanced angles; and the rhythm and flow of each line—but it is all easy, simple and natural.

This arrangement has elegance of height and style, bursting vitality, contrast and balance, and yet a most complete unity in the entire design. *Yang* and *Ying*, *In* and *Yo*, balance and contrast are conspicuous everywhere in this arrangement as they are in all well-made Japanese flower arrangements. Besides the qualities mentioned, it expresses beautifully the basic rule that each arrangement must present a moment of arrested growth in the life of a living plant.

What, therefore, the use of this law of contrast and balance did for Japanese floral art, it can do for us in creating an American floral art; that is, it can make us more conscious of other values in a plant than just the color or size of its blooms; it can show the beauty of the leaves belonging to the plant because they often have a delightful opposition of color between the upper and under sides as can be seen especially in the arrangement of *Aspidistra* or chrysanthemums. There is delightful charm in a tilted leaf. All these things add values untold to any flower arrangement; simple values to be sure, but effective values.

Chapter IX

Things Objectionable in an *Ikebana*

In 1688, a set of seven volumes on flower arrangement, the *Imayo Sugata,* or *Modern Fashions in Rikkwa,* was published in Kyoto. These volumes covered the art as it was known then. The author's name was not given. From this publication the following list of the common faults, "the errors to be avoided," has been taken.

Many of the cuts illustrating these errors were taken from one of a three-volume set on flower arrangement, the *Ikebana So-shi-an,* a *Short Guide to Ikebana,* published about 1750, of which I have a 1793 reprint. These illustrations naturally highly exaggerate the errors but also make them vivid.

1. Pigeon breast. An unpleasantly sharp angle.
   Fig. 109
2. Social climbing. "Man" must not rival "heaven."
   Fig. 110
3. Opposite branches must not be of equal length or too symmetrical.
   Fig. 111
4. Wall-poking branches, sticking out horizontally at back. Guest-poking branches, projecting towards the front. Heaven or earth-poking branches, projecting straight up or down.
   Figs. 112, 113
5. Earth pointing. All branches must turn upwards.
   Fig. 114
6. Both sides drooping in the same way.
   Fig. 115
7. Diseased, weak and frayed branches.
   Fig. 120
8. Under cutting. No crossing of branches is permissible.
   Fig. 116

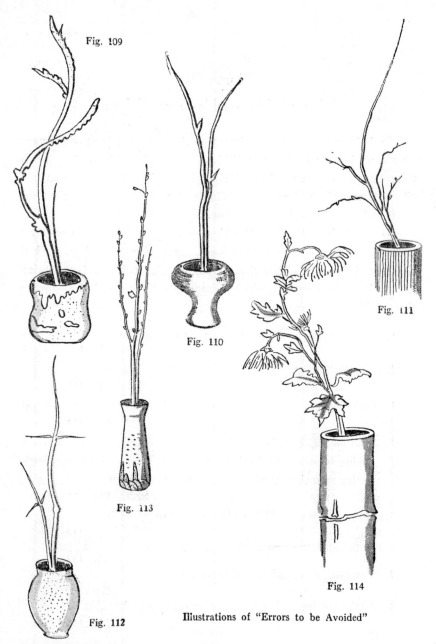

Fig. 109

Fig. 110

Fig. 111

Fig. 113

Fig. 112

Fig. 114

Illustrations of "Errors to be Avoided"

96

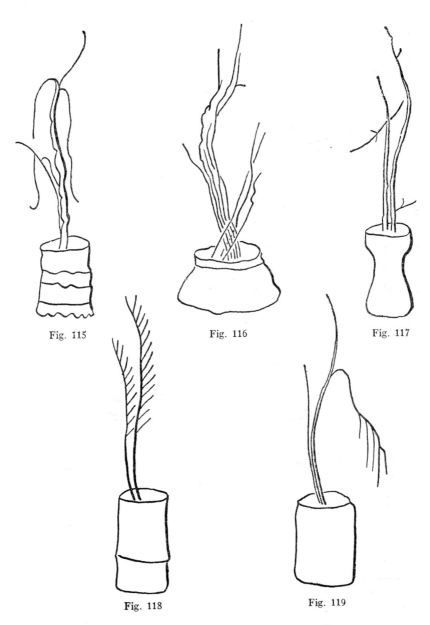

Fig. 115

Fig. 116

Fig. 117

Fig. 118

Fig. 119

Illustrations of "Errors to be Avoided"

9. View cutting. Another variety of the same thing.

Fig. 117

10. Leaves on one side only.

Fig. 118

11. Dead leaves, because they give a drooping and lifeless look.

Fig. 119

12. Sword leaves which stand out stiff and flat.

Fig. 121

13. Target flowers like bull's eyes.

Fig. 122

14. Stepped flowers, unpleasantly symmetrical.

Fig. 123

15. Equal sides. Lateral members should always be of unequal lengths.

Fig. 124

16. Boar's eyes. Flowers in regular, symmetrical clusters.

Fig. 125

17. Bent nail branch. Sharp, regular bends are not pleasing.

Fig. 126

18. Vase scraping. No part of the flowers may touch the vase.

Fig. 127

19. Color cutting or sandwiching. One color must not divide another alternately.

Fig. 128

20. One piece of foliage must not obscure another or a stem.

Fig. 121

All these rules are as good today as they were in 1688 and strongly stress the difference between good and bad form. Teachers of the classic art still instill their use in the minds of their students.

In addition to the above are some others that are as valuable:

Flowers must not face each other.

Flowers must not be hidden between leaves or stems.

Sword-shaped leaves must not have the sharp edge to the spectator.

There must not be an even number of large flowers.

All these rules are as good for ordinary bouquets as for Japanese flower arrangements.

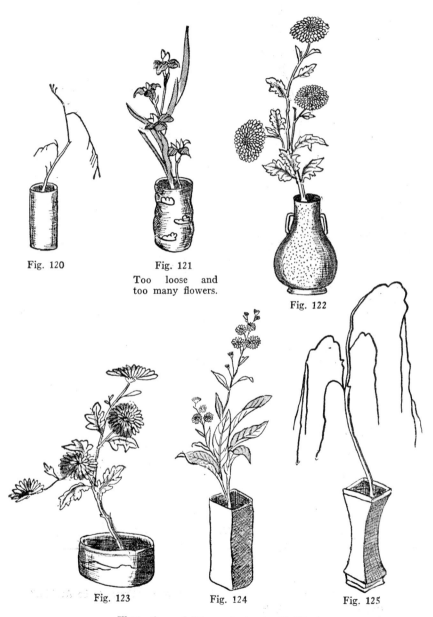

Fig. 120

Fig. 121
Too loose and too many flowers.

Fig. 122

Fig. 123

Fig. 124

Fig. 125

Illustrations of "Errors to be Avoided"

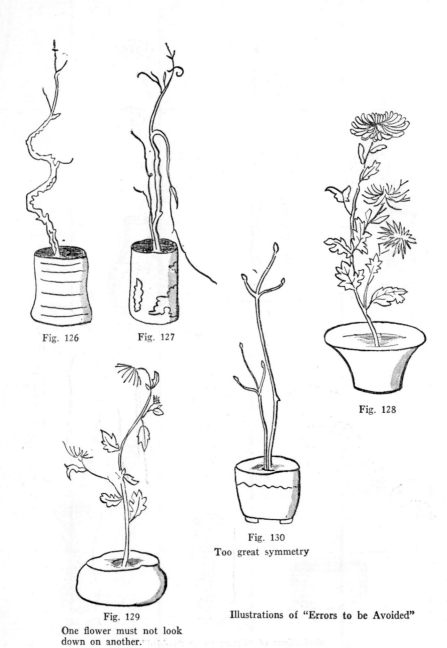

Fig. 126

Fig. 127

Fig. 128

Fig. 129
One flower must not look down on another.

Fig. 130
Too great symmetry

Illustrations of "Errors to be Avoided"

100

Chapter X

Technic

Flower arrangement technic has been routinized by the Japanese by twelve centuries of "cut and try," so they have no problems of containers, equipment and materials such as we, in America, have to consider; but we can routinize and systematize our technic and learn from them some well thought out fundamentals of the process.

The quickest way to learn anything is by visual instruction. Lacking a teacher, the next best way is by charts. For my classes I have enlarged (by means of a pantograph) each of the patterns on page 74 to a size fifteen inches long, on a sheet of white paper the size of a single page of newspaper. Each pattern chart can be hung up before the pupil by means of thumb-tacks. In that way each pattern gets into the pupil's mental equipment quickly because he can glance at it from time to time as he works. He does not have to stop to look in a book. The charts, needless to say, must be absolutely accurate.

Another most important detail is the necessity for working in a good light in front of a bare, plain wall space, where from time to time the material or the arrangement can be lifted or stood, so that one may get a clear silhouette, judge proportions, measure lengths of stems, get a slant on angles and to get a perspective on the work as it progresses. Glaring light from a window, clashing lines or figures distract and confuse the eye.

In the chapters on the equipment—materials, tools, wedges, *komi, kubari*—necessary to make an *ikebana* have been fully described, and it is a simple matter to spread the oilcloth on a large table where one has plenty of room to work.

A cylindrical container (Fig. 71) about ten inches high and three or four in diameter is the easiest shape to practice with and makes a perfectly satisfactory one for almost any room, or any material. Or a bulbous one

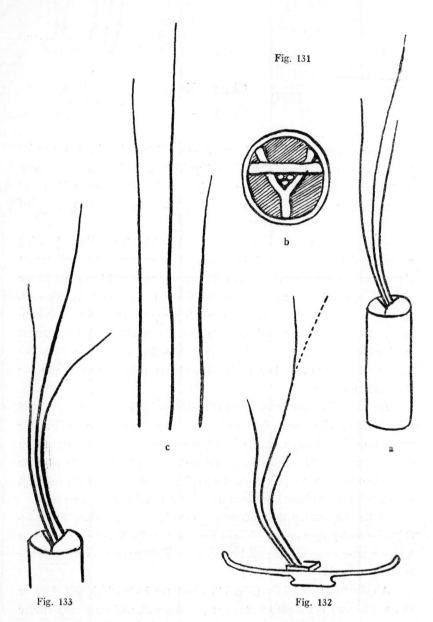

Fig. 131

b

c

a

Fig. 133

Fig. 132

Three stems and how to place them in a *kubari*

102

(Fig. 107) with an inserted tube can be used. Be sure that the inside of the tin tube or container (if pottery) has been roughened by cement. Place the container and other equipment on the right.

It is best to put out plenty of material, perferably long slender stems of red osier, privet or willow because these are easy to handle. The stems should be 36–50 inches long.

Until one has learned how to draw lines with stems it is wise to strip all leaves and flowers from the stems selected. Leaves and flowers at first are just a distraction and nuisance. Later on the many illustrations and practice will teach one how different flower materials may be used and where the flowers should be placed.

It is much better to start from the beginning with *long* stems until the real Japanese feeling for line, uncramped by prejudice or custom, is acquired. A tall arrangement gives a sense of freedom, a feeling of space, of being outside walls and away from one's self. A tall arrangement assumes importance and has to be given space (Fig. 40).

First fit the *kubari* in the container. Three slender stems do not need a wide *kubari;* a crotch with a spread of about an inch at the forked end when fitted should be wide enough. Lay the *kubari* across the top of the container, with the crotch a little off center so that the stem end is the shorter, and cut the *stem* where it crosses the *middle* of the rim so it will not be too short. Then insert the *kubari,* stem end first, about an inch below the rim and cut off the *forks* where they cross the rim. Put the *kubari* in the container and carefully fit the *kubari* into the container by lowering the stem end first and pulling up the forks to a level about an inch below the rim. Sometimes this fitting is difficult and tedious. Often one can use a bit of sandpaper in place of knife to rub off the end just the little bit needed to make a tight fit. A knife often takes off too much. It takes time to learn how to select the right size crotch and to make the crotch fit very tightly. Not only time but exact and patient care is necessary to remove the last tiny bit of woody stem that interferes with a fit so tight it takes considerable force to pull out. If the *kubari* is even a little loose it will not hold the stems firmly. When the *kubari* has been so well adjusted that only force can dislodge it and if the fork is neither too large or too small for the stems selected, we have gone a long way to the erection of a fine arrangement. The *kubari* should be inserted with the *forked ends* pointing towards the *back* of the container (Figs. 113a, 131b).

After the *kubari* has been fitted, select a slender but firm stem for the *komi*, or stay. A section of one of the discarded stems will be just right. Cut a length of the stem equal to the diameter of the container, just off center, that is just a little less than the actual diameter. The *komi* is to hold the stems firmly after they have been inserted in the *kubari* and is put across the *top* of the *kubari* forks (Fig. 131b). Lay this to one side.

Stand the container directly in front of you with *the forks at the back*. Do not change the position of the container while the arrangement is being made.

The Japanese floral artist always thinks of himself as standing *behind* the container. Therefore the arrangement is right or left of the person standing behind, though according to our standards these directions are reversed. The forks of the *kubari* should point *away* from you, the stem of it should point directly *towards* you. Since the *kubari* was cut with the stem end shorter than the forks, it allows the stems when inserted to rise from exactly the center of the container.

Follow the pattern indicated in Figure 87 because it is simple and requires little if any bending of stems. It is important to be able to make and fit a *kubari* and to try to get a good *nemoto*, and to have the stems in the right proportions in this first lesson.

Select from the various stems a heaven stem that is nicely graduated from end to tip; see if there isn't a stem with a slight curve, one that is long enough to reach to the bottom of the container and about thirty-three inches above the water line. Cut the end of this stem on a slant at the length indicated, or ten inches plus thirty-three inches, or the length of the container plus the length of the line, forty-three inches altogether (Cutting the end on a slant enables the stem to take up water.). Carefully remove all knotty or knobby places for a length of ten inches (length of container) plus five inches (length of *nemoto*) so that the stems may fit as closely together as possible. Each little knotty place hinders a close union. Each stem must be treated in this same careful way for the same distance.

Select for a man stem one that already approximates the slight curve of the man stem of the pattern and measure off a length about two thirds, or thirty inches of the length of the heaven stem; cut off the end of this stem slantingly. Remove all little knotty places as smoothly as possible up to the point of diversion (fifteen inches) the length of *nemoto* plus container length. Lay this stem beside the heaven stem. Select the earth stem, again taking one that somewhat approximates the earth line of the pattern. Cut the end slantingly at a length of one third the length of the heaven line and carefully smooth off the knotty, knobby points for the length of fifteen inches as was done for the other two stems.

The three stems or lines have now been selected and made ready to make the pattern, the floral design. They have been proportioned to the height of the average room, to the container and to each other, and to their own habit of growth. Clear away or put back into water for future use all material but these three stems.

Pick up the three stems, hold them in the left hand with the ends even, the heaven stem in front of the other two, so that the three stems form a triangle in the left hand, which holds them firmly. Grasp the three stems with the right hand (the left still holding them) *just below the point of diversion* and gently bend the three stems with the two hands so that the stems will have an inclination to stay together. Keep repeating the bending until they do have that inclination.

Now insert the earth stem into the *point* of the crotch of the *kubari* as tightly as possible. Next insert the heaven stem directly in front of the earth stem and the man stem on the other side of the heaven stem so that the three stems make a triangle that fits tightly in the triangle of the crotch (Fig. 131b). Hold each stem firmly as it is inserted and be sure that the tip of the heaven stem is directly above the center of the crotch. Pick up the *komi* with the right hand while still holding the stems firmly with the left and place it across the stems on *top* of the *kubari* so that it will make a tight stay for the stems (Fig. 131b).

The fact that the stems are long enough to stand on the bottom of the container aids in the firm erection of the arrangement as a whole. Fill the container with water sufficient to cover the *kubari.* This is the bare outline of the technic which takes patient care with each point outlined if one wishes to make a successful and correct arrangement.

If wedges are needed, which happens when the *kubari* is too large, make them the length of the container to the *kubari* plus an inch and a half (eleven and a half inches) and place them behind the three stems after the heaven, man, and earth stems have been inserted, and then place the *komi* as directed.

The making of this pattern (Fig. 87) and that of Figure 89 should be practiced over and over until one is absolutely sure of the curves. Then try them with more exaggerated curves such as in Figures 4, 5, 27, 28, 31 or differently proportioned lengths of man and earth (Figs. 52, 71, 82, 100).

After each design has been completed stand it and the pattern side by side in order to make an exact comparison. Nothing trains the eye so well as this constant lining up of pattern and arrangement.

It is interesting too, after a simple arrangement has been completed, to exaggerate each line by curving each stem. In order to do this without disturbing the lines, grasp the three stems with the left hand just below the *nemoto* (point of diversion) firmly, wet the fingers of the right hand and gently move them up and down the stem which is to be curved. Often even a little more curve in one stem or another makes a great difference in the grace and charm of a design.

For the other patterns the routine is the same up to the point where the three stems are made to follow a close union. Take up a stem suitable for a heaven line and compare it with the one shown in Figure 90. Determine the middle of the length from the point of diversion to within two inches of the tip (the last two or three inches of a main line are not usually taken into much account). Grasp the stem at this middle point

106

with *both* hands, thumbs close together on the *under side* of the stem, the two first fingers close together on *top* of the stem. Gently bend the stem as the fingers move slowly along the stem until within *two inches of the tip*. Treat the other half of the stem in the same way to the *point of diversion*. Repeat until the stem is bow-shaped, or it approximates the pattern. Do not try for too pronounced a curve for the first time. The last two inches of the stem, the tip end, should be bent back in the opposite direction, so that the tip should stand straight up and directly above the point where the stems emerge from the water (Figs. 104, 136, 140). See dotted line in Figure 132.

Pick up the heaven and man stems; hold them firmly with the left hand at the point of diversion; then with the wet finger and thumb of the right hand bend the man stem *out* and up the length of the stem until it approximates the pattern. When that stem line is satisfactory, go through the same process with the earth line. Some may find it easier to take each stem separately, beginning at the point of diversion, and bend it until it is in accordance with the pattern.

If this process is followed, special care must be taken to get a close union of stems. The insertion of the stems into the *kubari* is the same as in the process first described. After the stems are firmly fastened with the *komi*, if some slight adjustment of the stems seems desirable, *hold all three* stems tightly at the point of diversion with the left hand before attempting to make the adjustment. In that way one is sure not to upset or twist the arrangement. When an arrangement is to be moved or carried, or in the case of an arrangement made in a tube, hold the stems firmly *in this same way* and pick up tube or container with the right hand. The three stems must maintain their triangular and tridimensional form without shifting.

When a basin container is used, wedges are necessary to fasten the stems tightly. They should be inserted at the back of the stems so as not to show and should be cut off a very short distance above the *kubari*. In the basin container it is easy to make a mental calculation as to about how many and how long the wedges must be, from a glance at the size of the stems and the holder.

The holder must be heavy enough to hold the stems firmly. If one hasn't such a one but does have one right in other respects, a few dabs of plasticine can be affixed to the dry, under side of the holder and the holder applied to a *dry* basin. Another way to fix the holder firmly is to use parafin in the manner described on page 14. One of the heavy nuts shown on page 11 is very useful because of its weight and small core. The stems are inserted in a basket in a tube in the same triangular style as before described. The same patterns can be used in baskets as in other shapes. (Fig. 78). One does not always use as tall stems in a basin as can be put in an erect container but the *nemoto* should be the same. As has been before said, the length of the *nemoto* varies with the season and the material.

After the patterns have been pretty well learned, and some little skill has been attained in the use of bare stems, proceed with stems having leaves, followed later with stems having both leaves and flowers, *Weigela, Deutsia,* and any others obtainable.

The man line should always show a clean undersurface; that is, the leaves or flowers should cling to the upper part of the stem and not hang down *from* it (Fig. 135). This is also true of the earth line, which usually points more upward than the man line and is apt to follow the heaven line in mass and style (Figs. 52, 71). The *inside* of the bow of the heaven line is apt to have fewer leaves or flowers than the outside and the *front* of this stem must be its best looking side (Fig. 135). Each stem-line must be a cleanly defined line, not an interrupted or overloaded line (Figs. 24, 25).

In order to get a fine silhouette, leaves must often be thinned out on an arrangement. This must be done with great discrimination to leave a simple, natural effect, neither too many or too few (Fig. 39). The leaves should beautifully accent or thicken (shade) a line. The pedicels (stems) of both flowers and leaves often need a little bending to make them more easy, graceful, and natural. This is done by wetting the fingers and running them along the pedicel with gentle force.

Fig. 135

Notice that the leaves and flowers are on *top* of the man line.

Fig. 134

Patrinia or the "maiden flower" rises strongly and freely. The artist has caught "the moment of arrested growth" perfectly. Small stones are used over the flower holder.

The strength, style, and curve of the heaven line is just as important in the basin container because it aids in the appearance of vitality (Figs. 134, 135). The height, as the illustrations show, depends on the container and material.

There is a great tendency in the summer months to use basins, because it seems easier to use basins and because of the pleasant appearance of the water on a hot day. Summer arrangements in basins seem more expansive, as befits the season when all nature expands. Small stones may be put into basins to cover up anything useful but not beautiful and to make these arrangements more charming and credible. The dead black stones the Japanese use are very distinctive against the blue, gray, turquoise or white bottoms of pottery basins. The water in a basin should be as high as possible in the summer, a little less full in spring and fall. Stones, to be most effective, should be all of one color; traditionally white in summer, red in the fall, black in the winter, and green in the spring. They should be small—the Japanese use three sizes—but the most common is about half an inch in diameter. Do not use too many.

After an arrangement has been completed, stand it in a strong light with a plain, black wall space behind it so that every detail shows up in silhouette. If it is a practice arrangement of red osier, hang up the pattern beside it and carefully compare each line and angle with the pattern. It should be an exact copy. One needs to get a perspective on an arrangement as much as on a modeled statue. Look at your arrangement slowly, over and over again, each time with a special detail in mind, and satisfy yourself that *nemoto,* angles and proportions are satisfying.

Ask yourself whether the container harmonizes with the flower material (Fig. 26). Does the arrangement rise from the center of the container with vigor and strength? (Fig. 24) Are the angles at the point of diversion sharp and strong? (Fig. 28) Are the spaces between the lines well balanced? (Fig. 104) Are the lengths of the stem-lines well proportioned to the heaven line and to each other? (Fig. 52) Does the tip of the heaven line come just about over the base where the stems

emerge from the water? (Fig. 38)   Is the arrangement as a whole a satisfactory design? (Fig. 41)   Do the lines flow easily into space? (Fig. 71)
Is there a beautifully flowing rhythm? (Fig. 40)   These and many other
questions are answered in a fine arrangement.

In other words, look at the arrangement as if *you* had never seen
it before and someone else had asked you to judge these points.   Be
sternly critical.   It is the only way to learn flower arrangement, and to
train the eye to good form, strong easy line and correct detail.

Then go ahead and make another *ikebana*.

Chapter XI

Nejime

Nejime is the charming little cluster of small flowers often used in a flower arrangement of tree or shrub branches to make an arrangement less formal or to give a pleasing and vital contrast. A *nejime* takes the place of the earth stem, or stems, when there are more than three stems used. In Japan one of the most frequent uses of a *nejime* consists of two branches of evergreens with chrysanthemums for the *nejime*. The beauty, at least one of the beauties, of a *nejime* is the fact that as fast as one *nejime* withers it can be easily replaced with another of a different color and material while the evergreen stays fresh for two or three weeks. Chrysanthemums may be replaced by aster, small zinnias, narcissus, or calendula, a succession of colors and materials. Such an arrangement in the winter time is quite inexpensive, but very distinguished. More than that, low-growing plants may be used in a *nejime;* plants which would not otherwise be used in a Japanese arrangement.

A *nejime* consists of, let us say, three stems of chrysanthemums. The longest stem should be less than half the length of the heaven line and the other two stems in the same proportion to this longest stem as the man and earth lines are to the heaven line, so that the proportion of a *nejime* itself is very much that of an *ikebana* of full size. The stems are arranged in a triangular form, the longest stem nearest the evergreens, the shortest a little forward and between the other two.

The whole group should never look bunchy, as if a handful of flowers had been stuck in at the base, but as if they were gracefully growing at the roots of the tree. If the flowers are button chrysanthemums, there may be several on each stem. Larger flowers should be used more sparingly, with the blooms turned upward or slightly tilted forward (Fig. 137). The leaves of the *nejime* may be lower down than the point of diversion of the

112

Fig. 136

The artist could and did take advantage of any quirk of nature and made it say something. It is part of the value which is increased by the skilful artist. Height, proportion, balance, and contrast—all the desired values—are shown in this fine arrangement.

Fig. 137

A tall grass (*Miscanthus*) and a little *nejime* of gentian suggest August fields
and low places. The height, three and one-fourth times the container, shows
that it is late summer. Even such slightness of material has been made to
give full value and much beauty.

Fig. 139

This may be the branches
of almost any tree just
beginning to leaf out. The
nejime is made of chry-
santhemums.

Fig. 138

An evergreen with a charming
nejime of an unusual species of
cherry. The three stems are well
balanced and the contrast is
beautiful.

115

man and heaven stems. In other words the *nejime* has a point of diversion of its own which is lower than the point of diversion of the main *ikebana*. The *nejime* is inserted in the *kubari* close to the main stems but a little outward.

Chapter XII

The Final Placing of a Japanese Flower
Arrangement

In almost every magazine or newspaper are articles on the best and most harmonious ways of arranging the furniture in the room where the family life is centered; the best places for the lamps and lighting fixtures for the comfort of the eyes, or the best place to hang a fine painting. None of these things are done in a casual manner any more.

Therefore it ought not to seem an unnatural or difficult problem to select a spot in this room where a Japanese flower arrangement, or any other flower arrangement, may be placed and seen to the best advantage; a spot where a constant succession of flower arrangements may be seen; arrangements full of life and vigor, following the seasons and suggestive of many happy associations. Flower arrangements can keep us "in tune" with the coming and going of nature.

Japanese flower arrangements, to a remarkable extent, sharpen the eye and make the mind receptive to form, color, and plant growth. They enrich our daily lives and add to our appreciation of beauty When an arrangement has been well made, and well displayed, with nothing near it and nothing behind it to distract the eye or mind, it is as if a magnifying glass had been turned on something we had heretofore passed by, and had revealed some rarely lovely beauty that had been hidden from us.

Tranquillity emanates from a Japanese flower arrangement, too, and we begin "to play up" to the unspoken ideas that radiate from this living beauty. The whole house feels the influence of a fine Japanese flower arrangement, properly displayed. A photograph of a room containing a beautiful *ikebana* gives an effect far different from that of one with an ordinary arrangement in it, because the ordinary arrangement dependent on color and mass cannot have its glowing color projected by

Fig. 140

This arrangement of *Miscanthus* is even more simple than that shown in Figure 137 but it is a most delightful arrangement for a hot August day. The refreshing expanse of water is part of the arrangement. The basin is of cool grey celadon, much like crackle ware. The cool, soft greens and the dark stand underneath, the slight expectation of moving air, the upward thrust of the earth stem separated from the other two groups emphasizes the rigid lines of the container.

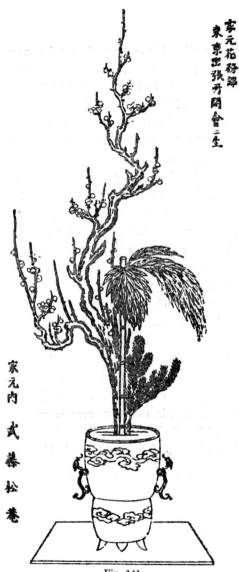

Fig. 141
"The three friends of winter"

A close study of this traditional New Year's arrangement will repay the student of Japanese flower arrangement. The beauty of it as a unit of design, the dignity of the container, and the height of the design, which would add alluring charm to any drawing room, are unusual, and yet in America there are materials which can be used in this same distinctive style.

119

a photograph mean much. If the place where a Japanese flower arrangement is displayed has a plain background and there are no accessories on the table on which it stands, and if the height of the arrangement is proportioned to the height of the room and the color adjusted to the colors in the room, it heightens and extends whatever charm the room has because its lines sweep into the lines of the room. These are details one takes care of with any furniture or decorative object.

Perspective must be given to a Japanese flower arrangement. Stand some distance away from an arrangement and look at it as if you had never seen the arrangement or the room before. If you judge the arrangement from the point of architectural proportion, a new feeling about flower arrangement will dawn on you, as to the effect of relationship, and the necessity for balance, contrast and proportion, in regard to arrangement and room. Look at a Japanese flower arrangement exactly as if it were a fine painting or statue and "hang" it accordingly, neither too high or too low, in order to get its full value.

In conclusion, no one who has ever gained even a slight knowledge of Japanese flower arrangement would ever go back to his state of ignorance because it has changed the face of nature for him. All through his garden he will see the lovely patterns he has been taught to copy. He sees day by day in the shrubs, in the trees, even in his window garden the lovely "heaven line" that he would like to snatch and put into a creation of his own, and enshrine as a focus of interest in his living room.

Glossary

Ashirai (Ah-shi-rye)   A group of three stems with small flowers to mak' a pleasing effect at the base of flowerless stems.

Daimyo (dye-myó)   Feudal lord.

Godown (go-down)   Fireproof storehouse a little separated from the house.

Hana (hah-nah)   Flower material or any kind of plant life.

Hi-den (He-den)   Secrets pertaining to flower arrangement.

Ikebana (Ee-kay-bah-nah)   *Ike* means to put in; *bana* or *han*a means flower material.

Kakemono (kah-kay-mo-no)   A hanging scroll picture.

Komi (ko-me)   A slender stem used as a stay to keep the stems firmly erect in an erect container.

Kubari (kuh-bah-re)   A forked twig used as flower fastener in an erect container.

Nejime (neh-ji-meh)   A little bunch of flowers used in the same way as an *ashirai*, in place of the "earth." It may be a little separated from the main stems.

Nemoto (neh-mo-to)   The close union of stems above the *kubari* to the point of diversion.

Shin-no-hana (shin-no-hah-nah)   Flowers used in worship of Buddha.

Rikkwa (reek-ka)   A kaleidoscopic view of a landscape.

Bibliography

—Western Language Works—

Averill, Mary. *Japanese Flower Arrangement* [*Ikebana*]. New York, 1914.

Averill, Mary. *The Flower Art of Japan.* New York: Dodd, Mead, 1923.

Church, A. H. "Japanese Vase Handles," *Portfolio,* vol. 23, London, 1892.

Clement, E. W. *The Japanese Floral Calendar.* Chicago: Open Court Publishing Co., 1911.

Conder, Josiah. *The Theory of Japanese Flower Arrangements.* Tokyo, 1889.

Du Cane, Florence and Du Cane, Ella. *The Flowers and Garden of Japan.* London: Adam and Charles Black, 1908.

Koehn, A. *The Art of Japanese Flower Arrangement.* Boston: Houghton Miffllin Co., 1934.

Nakashima, Taizo. "Philosophy of the Flower Arranging," *Far East,* vol. III, 1898.

Oshikawa, Mrs. Josui. *Shofuryu, Moribana, Nageire.* Tokyo, 1934.

Ohashi, S. *Shinzo Shirae, Japanese Flower Arrangement.* Tokyo: Yamanaka, 1935.

Preiniger, Margaret. *Japanese Flower Arrangement for the Modern Home.* Boston: Little Brown & Co., 1937.

Prenzill, Willi. "Der Blumen Kostlichkeit," *Asia Major,* Bd. 3, Berlin, 1926, pp. 357–380.

Pudor, H. "Die Japanische Blumenkunst," *Auf der Natur,* 1906.

Pudor, H. "Die Blumenkunst Japans," *Natur und Offenbarung,* 1907

Pudor, H. "Die Blumenkunst Japans," *Oesterreiche Monatsschrift fur die Orient,* 1913.

Revon, Michel. *De Arte Florali apud Japonenses.* Paris, 1896.

Sadler, A. K. *Art of Japanese Flower Arrangement in Japan.* New York: Dutton, 1932.

Shively, Lilian. "Japanese Flower Arrangement," *China Magazine,* Shanghai, 1935.

—Japanese Works—

Baran [*Aspidistra*] 44 paltes showing as many different ways of arranging *Aspidistra.* Osaka, Misho School, 1852.

Furiu-an So Sho. *Seikwa doku siu-ji-zai* [*Ikebana* self taught]. Principles of various schools, 6 vols. fully illustrated. Osaka, 1803.

Hiro Ho (?) *Sakura no nioi* [The Fragrance of the Cherry]. 61 illustrations. Osaka, Misho School, 1818.

Jiukyushi. *Rikkwa shodo shu* [The Right Principles of Rikkwa]. 3 vols. containing 107 very beautiful hand colored illustrations, "for the sole purpose of cultivating the Soul." 1684.

Ikenobo sen kyu. "Special Instruction in the Principles of The Flower Way House for use of the pupils of the Ikenobo School only, not for public sale." Reprint 1892. 118 Plates.

Nishiki-no-nusa [Old Brocade]. 98 Illustrations. Osaka, 1864.

Seikwa. Ikebana doku kai ko [*Ikebana* self taught]. By Sawada Hiroshi. 52 Illustrations. Osaka, 1892.

Seikwa. Ikebana hyaku-bin [100 designs in flower arrangement from the Ikenobo School]. 2 volumes. Tokyo, Ikenobo School, 1906.

Seikwa. Ikebana so-shi-an [Short Giude to *Ikebana*]. One volume only of a set of three. This volume principally concerned with "errors to be avoided." Vol. 2, 50 illustrations. Tokyo, 1822.

So-kwa [Flower Arrangement]. *Bi-shun no ye* [Descriptions of beautiful flower arrangements]. 105 illustrations. Osaka, 1891.

Yen Chu School of Flower Arrrangement. 1790. 17 illustrations.

Senden-sho. Vol. 12. [Lessons from Heavenly Sources] Kyoto, Nishimura Matazayemon, 1643. This is probably the oldest book on the principles of *Ikebana.* Author not known but a list of successive owners of this work given at the end of the book shows that these instructions were passed through 9 masters of the art during the years from 1445–1536.

Shinpan rikkwa shoshin sho [Manual of first lessons in Rikkwa]. Author not known. 1681.

Kokon rikkwa daizen. 5 volumes. Complete work in the ancient and modern forms with colored illustrations. Author not given. 1683.

Rikkwa imayo sugata [The Modern Fashions in Rikkwa]. 7 volumes. Names of Masters who designed the illustrations given in vol. 1–2, Vol. 3–4–5–6–7 contain secrets and directions of the art. Vol. 3 describes forms of branches of various trees. Vol. 4 gives technic of handling flowers. Vol. 5 is on flowering plants. Vol. 6 contains regulations and directions concerning finished forms of branches. Kyoto, 1688.

Rikkwa kinmo zui [An Illustrated Encyclopedia of Flower Arrangement]. 6 volumes. 1696.

Kokon zoho rikkwa daizen [Enlarged complete work on ancient and modern forms of Rikkwa]. 1 volume. Osaka, 1696.

Ikebana hiden zushiki [Illustrated Lessons on Secrets of Flower Arrangement]. Author Fukusai. Edo (Tokyo), Kikuya Kozaburo (publisher), 1798. This set of 5 volumes is very helpful and full.

The best of the books in the Library of Congress

Ikebana hayamanabi. Osaka, 1852. 10 volumes.
Ikebana tebiku gusa. Tokyo, 1800. 5 volumes.
Rikkwa jisei no yosooi. Tokyo, ca. 1800.

Sources of Illustrations

1. Frontispiece from "The Cha-no-yu, or Tea Ceremony" by W. Harding Smith, *Japan Society Transactions*, Vol. V, Plate 1.

2. a. Fig. 3 from Vol. 1 and
   b. Figs. 1 and 2 from Vol. 2 of *Rikkwa Shodo Shu* by Jiukyushi, 1684.

3. Figs. 4, 26, 27, 35, 36, 37, 38, 52, 54, 68, 96, 101, 102, 103, 136, 137, and 141 from *Ikenobo sen kyu.* Reprint 1892.

4. Figs. 103–130 from *Seikwa, Ikebana So-shi-an* Vol. 2. 1822.

5. Figs. 24, 25, 39 from *Nishiki-no-nusa.* 1864.

6. Figs. 41, 51, 55, 140 from *So-kwa. Bi-shun no ye,* 1891.

7. a. Figs. 19–23 from Vol. 1 of *Seikwa doku shiu-ji-sai* by Furiu-an So Sho, 1893.
   b. Figs. 28, 29, 30, 31, 34, 42, 43, 81, 85, 86, 93, 94, 95, 99, 108 from Vol. 2.
   c. Figs. 32, 44, 72, 77, 78, 79, 80, 98, 100, 106 from Vol. 3.
   d. Figs. 4, 5, 33, 47, 69, 70, 134 from Vol. 4.
   e. Figs. 46, 48, 83, 84, 97, 104, 105, 107, 135 from Vol. 5.
   f. Fig. 45 from Vol. 6.

8. a. Figs. 49 and 71 from Vol. 1 of *Seikwa Ikenobo hyaku-bin,* 1906.
   b. Figs. 40, 50, 76, 82, 138, 139 from Vol. 2.